Preface

I wrote this book to break the silence around something many men experience but rarely talk about: how childhood sexual abuse can leave a man confused about his sexual identity.

At thirteen, I was sexually abused for two years by a man tied to my family—an ordeal that combined with other childhood trauma, derailed my growth and left me uncertain of who I was. Healing felt like an impossible climb—not because I wasn't strong enough, but because I had no language or examples to understand what had happened.

In most cultures, male sexual trauma, especially when it touches sexual identity, remains hidden behind stigma. Labels like straight, gay, or bi didn't clarify things for me; they only deepened the confusion. In psychology, it's well known that trauma can scramble sexual identity, yet most people outside the field remain unaware of it. Many assume that arousal toward a particular gender defines orientation, when in reality, trauma can distort arousal patterns in ways that have nothing to do with a person's true identity.

Male sexual abuse is far more common than most people think. The CDC estimates that approximately one in six U.S. men has experienced some form of sexual violence in his lifetime, and about one in 13 report such abuse occurring during childhood — and those figures reflect only the cases that are reported.

Most of us learn early that there's no safe place to share what happened. When we do try, we are often met with discomfort, disbelief, or silence.

The world insists men must be invulnerable—always in control, always wanting sex, never violated. That leaves little room for men harmed as boys. For many of us, abuse stalled the body's natural development; our nervous systems never fully wired a confident, felt sense of maleness. By maleness, I don't mean roles or expectations, but an embodied experience—the primal, physical sense of being male that precedes conscious thought and is registered by the nervous system. Our bodies grow and look whole, but inside we are stuck in boyhood—improvising workarounds for stalled growth.

When sensation is cut off from a specific part of the body, the mind has no way to register that area as part of the self. In cases of sexual abuse, the nervous system often pulls the plug on the very area that was violated. For example, if a man cannot physically feel his genitals—if he lacks a steady, grounded sensation of his own phallus or testicles—his brain loses an important anchor. He is left trying to navigate manhood while numb in his own pelvis. Without that physical, felt sense of his anatomy, it can become difficult to feel like a man, leaving him vulnerable to confusion about who he is and who he is attracted to.

"Trauma is not what happens to us, but what we hold inside in the absence of an empathetic witness," writes somatic therapist Peter Levine. For many men, that witness never appears. We carry the pain alone, without words or reflection. But when real empathy—not pity or analysis—finally arrives, everything can change. It gives form to what was once unspeakable, brings trauma-shaped nervous system patterns into awareness, and helps turn unnamed pain, long held in shame, into a life worth living.

I'm sharing my story for men who were sexually abused as boys and are struggling to understand what's happening inside them. If reading this helps even one person feel less alone, then I've done what I set out to do.

This book isn't about sexual orientation; it's about trauma. I respect everyone's right to live their sexuality freely. My story doesn't defend straightness or question gayness. The same-sex encounters I describe could just as easily have involved women if my abuser had been female. Gender isn't the issue—trauma is.

I offer these pages as reflection, not prescription. Healing is personal and creative. If anything I write resonates, let it guide you to follow your own path and take the steps your body is ready for. If you pursue similar work, do so with a licensed somatic therapist. I want you to thrive—and, above all, stay safe.

This memoir traces my healing, not my whole life. The path wasn't linear—it spiraled, stalled, and doubled back. For clarity, I've arranged the story as waypoints along that path.

What follows is drawn from my memory and interpretation, offered in hopes of deepening our understanding of trauma. In some places, events are condensed, combined, or told symbolically to reflect their emotional truth rather than a literal chronology. All names have been changed, and some places and identifying details have been altered or generalized to protect privacy. What is preserved throughout is the truth of my experience.

You'll notice somatic—body-based—language throughout. My healing draws on somatic psychology, but I'm not proving a theory; I'm telling the story as I lived it. For deeper insight into how the nervous system senses safety and threat outside awareness, see neuroception, a term coined by neuroscientist Stephen Porges. Operating beneath consciousness, neuroception guides whether we connect, flee (fight), fight, appease (fawn), or freeze. When threat is overwhelming, protection can take the form of dissociation—forgetting, numbing, or narrowing what we feel. Dissociation is a physiological threshold, the body's way of protecting itself when experience exceeds capacity. For a thoughtful exploration, I recommend Donald Kalsched's Trauma and the Soul.

Some parts of this memoir are hard to read. They show the emotional and physical reality of childhood trauma. If at any point you feel overwhelmed, please pause, breathe, and return when you're ready. Your well-being matters.

Contents

Poisoned Soil

1967

Chapter 1

Lahore, Pakistan

Mughal domes spear a diesel sky while barefoot children thread between Mercedes and donkey carts. Dust, jasmine, sewage, incense: the air refuses to choose sides. Rag-roofed huts lean against walls crowned with iron spikes; diplomats' limousines idle beside beggars' mats. Women in flowing black burqas bargain beside others in neon saris slung low, midriffs bare, stilettos clicking.

On a street in Lahore, a bell clangs above a shopkeeper's door, its sound spilling into the street. I am three, standing with my cousins—Ali, Bil, and Rafi—four boys all born within a year of each other. A cloud of cardamom sugar blooms around us as we walk inside, sweetness rising at the back of my nose and sliding down my throat; my mouth floods.

"Anything you want," Uncle Jamal says, sweeping his hand over the glass jars.
Ali, Bil, and Rafi lunge—orange peel drops, rose toffee, fists of lemon rock.
My shoulders hitch forward, the lunge rising like my cousins'—then lock.
Arms pin to my sides.
Toes grip my dusty flip-flops.

"Why not you?" Uncle Jamal asks, crouching to meet my eyes. "Mommy doesn't let me eat candy."

I swallow hard.
The burn behind my eyes dries.
Anger sparks in my chest—smolders to ash.
No protest. No tears.

He leans in closer. "I'll talk with her," he says. "Children should have some freedom."

The place in my body where want lives can't find a way out. Over time it calcifies, seals off. I feel only absence where desire should be.

My father's master's degree bought us houses behind brick ramparts. Marble floors lie cool as river stone. Hedges stand clipped into cubes. The water runs glass-clear. Ours is a moderate Muslim household—we pray if we wish, fast if we choose, dress as we like. My parents' marriage was arranged—she twenty, he twenty-five—and they first saw each other on their wedding day. Both were village-born, but Mother had no schooling. From the start, the gap in their education is a door closed between them.

On the surface, I have everything a boy needs to be free. Yet I am stuck—rules cinch my breath beneath my collarbones, ribs clamped. Mother controls the menu, the clock, my playtime—and me.

She vets every neighborhood kid I might play with,
pulling each aside: "Not too rough." Before long they
laugh—"mommy's boy"—and shut me out.

Still, they can't stamp out every want; one waits by my shoes.

At four, I sway in the car's back seat at night. A tin of
rasgullas—cheese balls in rose-water syrup—glows by my feet.
It presses against my shins, cool and still, like a treasure chest. I
lift the lid. One velvet orb melts on my tongue—then another,
then a third.
By the time the car sighs at our gate, the tin is empty. I set the
lid back on, and laughter fizzes in my chest. My parents crack
it open, astonished—then let their giggles spill into mine.

Pakistani patriarchy was brutal: men worked; women kept
house. Sons were counted as wealth; daughters as debts paid
in dowry. A wife with only girls could be put away like a
cracked clay pot—divorce cheap, no alimony, no child support.
Before me, my parents had five daughters—two sets of twins
and another girl; one set died at a month old. Sixteen years
into their marriage, I arrived, the boy: proof my father's name
would march on, and my mother's worth would hold.

Even as a boy, patriarchy cost me.

One Saturday morning, at sixteen, I stop by my neighbor
Omar's. Cricket commentary crackles from the TV; a sweating
pitcher of lemonade sits on the coffee table. On the couch,

all three of them are in pajama pants and shirts—father in
the middle, Omar leaning on one side, his little brother on
the other. Their father drapes an arm around each boy, eyes
never leaving the screen. Pakistan scores: he whoops, kisses the
younger one's temple, squeezes Omar's shoulder. Just a dad on
a couch with his boys.

Color slides out of my face; an ache too big to feel rises under
my sternum. The room keeps roaring for Pakistan, but a young
voice cuts through: *Why don't I have a single memory of my
father's arms around me?* A question I've carried for as long as
I can remember.

Omar tugs me to a board game; I smile on cue, hollow inside.
At dusk I walk home down the dusty street.

I step through our gate and find my mother with her sisters,
Shazia and Fozia, talking in the front yard and sipping tea. I
take the empty chair and prop my feet on the brown cane table.

The question is still lodged in my throat.
"Why don't you ever answer me?" I ask Mother. "Why doesn't
Father love me?"
"He doesn't love anyone," she says.
"That doesn't explain why he saves his coldest silence for me."

Aunt Shazia traces the rim of her cup, then meets Mother's eyes.
"He's old enough. You should tell him."

Mother looks at the garden lattice. Twice she starts a sentence,
lets it die.

"I'll tell you," she says. Her voice low, steady.

"Soon after we wed, your father kept a polished, educated woman on the side. When I was pregnant with you, he said that if it wasn't a boy, he'd leave me for her and throw me and the girls out. You were born a boy, and that saved us."

My mother sobs. Her sisters fold around her.
I hold my breath.

"That's why I made sure you stayed safe and healthy."

Then Mother, quieter: "He wouldn't touch you for three years. Said you'd cost him the woman he wanted."

Crushed.

When grief settles, I ask, "I thought he wanted a boy. Shouldn't he have loved me more?"

"I wish I understood your father well enough to explain," Mother says. "He keeps looking for reasons to be angry, to dominate. After you were born, he left the other woman—maybe he missed her and blamed you. I don't know."

What I feel has a name: father hunger.
That ache keeps me scanning for a father in other men, leaving me open to those who know how to exploit it.

That hunger threads through the role my parents drafted me into—I am not a child born into their marriage; to my mother I am insurance, to my father, status. That script sinks in until I act it out without thinking.

Chapter 2

Ages Birth to Six

Heat shimmers over the stream as we queue on the sunbaked rock, five-year-olds chanting for the next launch. Ali flies first; water fizzes, soda-cold, and we roar. One by one we jump—each splash pearling our shins. When my feet meet the smooth pebbles, coolness slides upward, bubbling toward a grin I can't swallow. Rafi surfaces, spitting laughter; Bil punches a fountain skyward, the whole stream turning to light.

Bare feet slap the dusty path home, mud flaking from our legs like old paint. No gates, no boundary walls—only earthen houses leaning into the lane, cousins blooming there like marigolds. Cowbells clang from the next field. We lock elbows—Ali to me, me to Rafi, Rafi to Bil—a four-boy-chain hauling uphill, pledging a life of orchard adventures and sleepy time secrets.

At the rise, Uncle Jamal's spread appears: a low, broad farmhouse of sun-browned clay, flanked by wheat stubble, vegetable rows, and a cowshed heavy with hay. The courtyard well sings as a bucket creaks up, droplets pattering against brick.

Girls chalk hopscotch squares just inside the gate—their feet barred from the stream that drenches us wild. Adults stay hypervigilant about dangers for girls—especially sexual ones—keeping them close, every errand chaperoned. For boys, silence; risks go unnamed.

That morning was more than a visit. Two hours on a broken highway in our Fiat jolted us out of Lahore's Westernized enclaves and into our rural village near Sialkot. It's where my parents grew up—largely untouched by the West. Most of my uncles, aunts, and cousins live here. My father is the outlier; his quick mind carried him into British-run schools in colonial India before the Partition split the country into India and Pakistan. That path later pulled him toward Lahore—Pakistan's second-largest city.

In our village, relatives sleep on rooftops and measure status by the sweetness of their well water. In Lahore, my father gleams like a regimental badge—polished English, polished shoes, quick to clip away any village habit clinging to our name. My mother follows, uneasy in her new heels; the rest of the kin stay barefoot, free, faintly amused.

The next day, Aunt Yasmeen calls, "Wash—lunch is ready!" The scent of sizzling ghee drifts under the neem tree's umbrella.

Twenty of us sit cross-legged on a worn floral cotton sheet, daikon radish *parathas*—my favorite—steaming in the center. Bowls of *raita* and jaggery orbit like small moons, the radish's peppery scent pricking the noon heat. Laughter weaves through the circle.

Mother stills it.
"Where's my prince's chicken? He needs protein—I asked for it."

Silence sinks. My hand freezes as I tear the paratha; steam kisses my knuckles and vanishes. Around the sheet, cousins study their plates—polite, careful, not knowing where to look. Aunt Yasmeen forces a smile. "Faraz is blessed—may every child be so lucky." Plates clink as she stands. "I'll fetch his chicken. How could I forget—I bought it fresh this morning."

She slips into the kitchen, the silence that follows thickens. Mother sets her hand on the back of my neck—warm at first, then heavy. "My boy," she murmurs—tender, warm. The caress repeats; each pass presses me flatter.
Thinner.
Invisible.

Aunt Yasmeen returns with chicken—a village luxury—sets it on my plate. Around the circle, eyes touch and slip away, envy tucked behind good manners, their own plates holding the humble, everyday parathas and raita.

I break a piece of the chicken and swallow. It lands like a rock in my stomach.
Eyes fixed on me, burning.
My breath goes shallow.
Body thins to an outline.
A thought flickers: *Something is wrong with me.*
It cools into fog, sinks to my belly, sets like stone.

Uncle Jamal cracks a joke. Mother and Father laugh with the rest.

Later that afternoon, the courtyard dozes after lunch—uncles on woven rope beds, aunts shelling peas in slow rhythm. We slip out the side gate: Rafi first, then Bil, Ali, and me, bare feet whispering over cracked earth. The mango trees wait like ladders of green-gold. We scramble up, giggling each time a sap-slick fruit thuds to the ground. My palms are resin-sticky when the branch under me lurches.

Slip. Drop. Impact.

Air punches from my ribs; light splinters white. A cry tears loose.

Footsteps thunder. Mother wails. Hands—too rough, too many.
Heat, noise.

The grown-ups argue over who let the boy—me—fall. Mother barks at my cousins—"Watch my son! No more rough play." Her face crumples; no one answers.

On later visits, they obey.
Rafi offers me the lowest branch; Ali moves aside when we run; Bil's laughter stalls if I stumble. They still love me, but each game feels padded, the risk vacuum-sealed. I hate their new caution more than the bruises.

I become the boy made of glass.

———————————————

Still, I don't fully lose myself. I keep small resistances—a quieter kind of bravery I don't yet have words for.

Weeks later, a neighbor crouches to my height.
"What will you be when you grow up?"
"A fighter pilot," I say. The radio keeps crackling with news of jets and war with India.
She smiles. "And what will you do?"
"I'll fly fast," I say, and I make a little whooshing sound that makes her laugh.
"Why?"
"So I can go anywhere I want. To Sialkot, to the moon."

The lane hums: a pressure cooker hisses, someone calls for tea, a kite tugs its string. For a while, that is enough.

Later that year in Lahore.
I am on the living room rug, fitting Meccano girders into place. Screws whisper, gears lock together, the half-built crane rising steady and true. Hours pass in a single, unbroken hum.

A bolt sticks.
I carry the half-built crane to Father, hidden behind his newspaper, a wall between us.

"Daddy, can you help me tighten this?"
The paper doesn't move. His voice—flat, distant.
He looks at Uncle Jamal, in town for a visit.
"Jamal, give the boy a hand."
Uncle's eyebrows lift.
Father folds the pages, stands, walks out.
No look. No word. Only the cold draft of the AC trailing him down the hall.

That evening.
Father is out on a business dinner, so the table belongs to
Mother, the girls, and me. With Father, dinners clench silent;
tonight our tongues loosen. Mother doesn't cook—leftovers fill
the pot, cumin scent rising.

The twins—Nimra and Huma, fifteen—lean into each other,
their bright bangles chiming as they chatter about the clothes
of movie actresses.
"Zeba," Nimra says, tossing her hair. "No one wears a sari
better."
"Shabnam's dresses turn more heads," Huma shoots back.

Their laughter braids with the clink of plates until Mother cools
it with a glance. "Good looks won't cook your meals. After
high school, you'll go to Home Economics College—learn to
run a house." The twins nod.

Ashi, nine—quiet and sharp—sits with a pencil behind her
ear, notebook hugged close. Homework done, she eats in
small bites, gaze steady. Teachers praise her; at home, silence.
Girls' education doesn't matter—their worth is measured by the
husbands they marry.

Mother's hand lingers on my shoulder as she serves. The
bowl holds too little; she chooses the largest piece of beef for
me, dividing the rest among the girls. Heat slips through the
room—eyes to plate, plate to me.
"Why does he get all the attention?" Huma says.
Nimra doesn't look up. "We all know why."

———————————

14

Six months later, another Sialkot run begins under a sky as flat as old bone.

Father drives; Mother rides shotgun, purse in her lap. My three sisters and I line the backseat—knees touching, heads tipping together each time the Fiat bounces a pothole.
The city thins to scrub and heat. Fifteen minutes out, Father speaks without turning.

"Did you lock the house?"
Mother nods yes.
"Keys?"
Mother opens her purse—soft rustle. She keeps digging—breath hitching. One side pocket, then another. No jingle. Her skin blanches.

Father's hand drums the steering wheel.
"Keys."

She tries again, fingers moving faster, breath shorter. Empty lining. Panic.
Her face tightens. I feel it before I see it, a silence that fills the car like smoke.

Then the strike.
Voice—loud, razor-sharp.
"Either get some brains—"
Road hum swallows the words—
"—or die."

Again.
And again.
Each repetition lands like a hammer on the same cracked plate.

I don't look at Mother. I watch the rearview mirror instead, catching flashes of Father's eyes—steady on the road, bright with a satisfaction I can't name.

On our moonless return from Sialkot, night presses close. Kiln-hot wind sweeps grit through the Fiat's high-beam tunnel.

Mother and Father argue about something I don't remember. Voices overlap, climb, break apart like brittle glass. The noise claws my skin. I press my fists to my ears.

"Stop—please stop. I want to die!"

The car jerks. Brakes squeal. Gravel spits. Father's voice: flat, surgical. "Get out."

Door hinge groans. I slide onto the shoulder—dust-powdered sandals, trembling calves. Door slams. Engine revs, tail-lights flare. They drive away.

No cars. No buildings. No voices—just scrub grass and a pulse in my ears, fluttering like an autumn leaf clinging to its branch.

Minutes stretch. Heat slides off. Silence seeps in—thin, then thicker—until the pond across the road holds the whole night like dark glass. *Let them stay gone*, I think.

A breeze combs the grass. My chest rises once—again—steady now. Something under my ribs unknots. The quiet doesn't crush; it cradles.

I don't know how long—maybe ten minutes—headlights skim the brush. Mother runs to me, brushes grit from my hair and presses my forehead to her talcum-scented belly. Father waits by the idling Fiat, the engine's hum climbing into my legs as I slide onto the vinyl seat.

My father's cruelty doesn't make me in his image; my skin recoils at taking his shape. No model there—only hunger.

Overprotection fences me off from cousins and sisters until the games go on without me. I grow up feeling delicate, wrong, built to disappear.
My mother's warnings to my playmates to be gentle, and her panic over every small injury, make me feel guilty—what I want makes her feel bad. My body learns to wait for her cues, to want only what she allows.

When school begins, I have no armor. The impulse to play, to act on my own—the instincts needed to belong among schoolchildren—never reach my muscles.

Chapter 3

Ages 6 to 12

Father's work often lifts us out of Lahore's fumes and sets us where the fields breathe. He maintains the irrigation canals—gates, culverts, embankments—and is allowed to take his family along on inspection drives. At six, I watch our new sky-blue Mazda bump off the rutted highway and nose toward Tarbela Rest House.

When we arrive, it feels both familiar and grand—like so many guest houses we've stayed in. A wide courtyard holds a turquoise pool that breaks the sky into shifting fragments. High ceilings meet clerestory vents where the hot air slips out; the rooms stay cool. The place sits on a hill, terraced lawns stepping toward the view—green edges giving way to a sunlit horizon where the Indus River curls like a silver ribbon.

I drift to the lawn. The grass cools my feet; eucalyptus sweetens the air; a breeze puffs my shirt like a small sail. One deep breath and the tightness city air leaves in my chest loosens.

As in many old colonial guest houses, the cooks still make European-style meals. I am already picturing my favorite: roasted chicken with potatoes and trifle for dessert. I love everything about trifle—the way the sponge cake drinks up syrup, the way the jelly wobbles under the fruit, the cool sweetness of the cream on top. Each spoonful is a layered surprise, a slow unfolding of texture and taste that feels playful and complete.

Season after season we return, and each visit works the same quiet magic on my body: knots slip, lungs fill, the world feels easier.

And each time, I tell myself: *The Indus holds steady—so will I.*

But rivers don't fit in lunchboxes, and the Indus can't walk with me to school. By the time monsoon clouds sink over Lahore, the river is only an afterimage—turquoise drained to gray—while a different kind of water pools in my stomach each morning.

Around my sixth birthday, my parents enroll me at Baby Angelic, a private academy within walking distance of our gate. The name, all English sugar, tastes strange against the diesel air. They press a uniform into my hands: gray shorts, a red dress shirt, a plastic belt that squeaks when I breathe.

The school pavement radiates heat; chalk lines ghost it like scars. Bodies hurtle into games I can't name—thuds, yelps, a river of laughter. I hover at the edge, knees locked, knuckles whitening around the lunch tin Mother packed. Every jostle of the crowd sends a ripple through my skin as if my bones are learning to flinch.

I try counting—one Indus, two Indus—to slow my heart, but the river's calm doesn't come. Metal pools behind my teeth; bodies press in, cloth scraping against cloth, loud as a warning.

The other boys move like a single animal with a hundred legs;
I can't read its intentions. It doesn't turn, doesn't apologize.
It simply keeps running, and I stand there in my brand-new
brightness—red shirt, gray shorts, stiff as a traffic sign—unable
to find the moment when boys learn how to belong.

They know the code, a small voice whispers, and you are
dreaming rivers.

The moment class lets out, the playground dissolves into
another rush of elbows and metal lunch tins. Two older boys
peel me from the edge of the crowd as neatly as tangerines from
their skins.

Elbows, lunch tins, heat.
My feet leave the ground. One boy behind, locking my arms.
Another in front, grin too wide.
Fist. Gut. Darkness.
Air won't come. Colors wash to static.

Next day—
Same grip, quicker. Lock. Hit. Release.

Day three—I hide inside myself. Small. Quiet. Easy to grab.
Easier to hurt.

Mother? Father? The thought never sparks.

My body speaks instead.
Dawn. Ice skin. Stomach jackknifes. Vomit. Rinse. Repeat.

Mother's palm on my forehead. "No fever. You'll be late."

Pavement underfoot. Collar wired with static. Sick again at the gate.

A week of this and the grown-ups blink.
Father—"lost workdays." Mother—"evil eye."
Solution: pull the boy; push him somewhere new.

———————————

We visit Anarkali Bazaar the following year. Men walk hand in hand—wrists easy, shoulders touching. Across the lane, a wife reaches to straighten her husband's collar; Mother's grip tightens. "Vulgar," she says, eyes flat.

Affection between men passes without comment, always assumed platonic. Any tenderness between men and women stays out of sight—even parents never show it around their children. All I know is that men can be tender with men—never with women. I know nothing of sexual acts—whether between men and women or among men; that part is blank on my map.

Later that year, my mother's youngest brother, Yousaf, arrives. He is twenty-five, an auto mechanic in Karachi; the distance keeps him away most years, which is why a whole week with us feels like a holiday. He plays with me all week, sprinting across the yard like a boy. In our family, he is the gentle one—soft-spoken.

One evening we sit on the veranda, Mother's fingers drifting through my hair.
Uncle Yousaf folds himself cross-legged on a cane chair, knees

in tidy triangles, smiling at nothing.

Ping. Mother's spoon strikes porcelain. My head dips with the sound.

"I'd like you to grow up like your uncle Yousaf, not your father," she says, her thumb pressing my crown.

"When tempers flare, he stays quiet. And when women pass, his eyes stay low."

Her palm settles firmer on my head—a lid over water about to boil.

The brick pattern beneath my feet sharpens: red, black, red—safe squares if I stay inside the lines.

Shrink the voice. Lower the gaze. Keep limbs folded small.

Across the lawn, Yousaf beckons with a soft whistle—"Race?"

Mother's hand loosens. "Go," she allows.

I run—feeling the leash of her gaze as the wind cools my cheeks.

Another lesson, another attempt to domesticate me.

———————————

At age ten, one of the twins, Nimra, is married off at twenty. It's an arranged match: her husband is thirty, a pharmacist in New York. Like my parents, the first time they meet is on their wedding day. That morning she stands behind the window, watching a dented Suzuki deliver the stranger who will take her to America. "I don't like him," she whispers to Huma, while downstairs the *dholak* keeps celebrating—its drumbeat cheerful, unstoppable. Shortly after the wedding, she leaves for New York and, within two years, gives birth to two boys.

She chooses to remain a housewife in the United States, her world circling around husband, children, and home.

In a country full of opportunities, she keeps to a small, conservative Pakistani circle. Admired for her looks, she pours her energy into clothes—Bollywood styles copied, each new trend an impressive mask. The wardrobe grows; her world stays narrow, as if she never left Lahore.

On my twelfth birthday, Uncle Jamal rolls out a bike—red as fire, handlebars spread like wings, the seat just high enough to invite a jump.
My first shove at the pedals wobbles, the next holds; by sunset I'm a crimson streak carving loops, chasing trails beneath a sky as big as forever.
Oak tree shadows drum my shins; hoopoes loft ahead, crests bright as signal flags. Wheat stubble crackles under the tires, then gives way to open ground that unrolls like a promise—nothing but earth, horizon, and the silence between.
Spokes, sky—no vigilant eyes. I pedal until dusk stitches violet seams across the fields, and the wind—dust, marigold, distant canal water—lifts every thread of dread from my skin.
Bats lift, and the first star pins itself above the neem trees.
Each ride becomes a wordless prayer: let motion be freedom.
The trails grant it—miles of innocent questions, a rolling hush I fill with breath and let loosen whatever tightens.

We rarely see our cousins past elementary school. Aunts and uncles grew busy with their own families. School and home are the only spaces for friendship and play.

There, fear runs my days—most things, most people. Home is a puppet stage; rules pull the strings, my parents hold the crossbar.

The school corridors are gauntlets; teachers' sticks splinter desktops; laughter peels away my last layer of defense. Bullying and beatings are routine. I have no friends—only brief talks with the few boys the bullies pick on. I keep to the margins; the margins keep me safe.

I practice invisibility the way other children practice spelling:

Hold breath. Fold shoulders. Mute voice.

Erase the boy.

Shortly after my twelfth birthday, I sit at the edge of the schoolyard, dust biting at my ankles; the boys' shouts rise and break like waves.

In the center, seven flat stones stack on the dirt. A boy hurls a tennis ball—crack—the pile bursts. Some sprint to rebuild, others chase the ball to smash it again. The game is *Pitho Gol Garam.*
Feet blur. Arms fling. Laughter bursts open.

My body hums. I want what moves them to move me. I feel it rising—the current that runs through a group like a single breath.
The wanting is sharp. But I've never played with a group. Fear

presses in. Tears sting.
My thighs twitch to spring. Breath swells too big for my ribs.
I want to be in the circle—noise, sweat, laughter.

Some exiled instinct whispers: *Go now. Belong.*
I join the circle.

A scuffed ball lifts into noon light—a creamy arc against a cobalt
sky—and I grab it.
I step forward and throw it at the stones.
I miss—my arm too loose, baby arc, the ball dying short.

Silence vacuums the yard.
Thirty boys close in, the ring tightens.
"*Khusra, khusra—hijra,*" they jeer—neither real man nor real
woman.

Heat—ice—heat.
Air, gone.
Vision tunnels to dust motes.
Sound dims
My body slips its moorings.

I float inches above my shoes, watching a paper-cutout boy
blink at ground that will not hold him.
No tears. No protest.
Only the slow, granular re-coagulation of shame around a
name that is not mine.

Evening in my room. Mirror practice—ball in fist.
Throw.
Elbow higher.
Throw.

Wrist locked.
Months of this: grafting a man onto my sapling frame, terrified
one crooked angle will stunt the tree.

Next day.
Huma's radio spills a song I've never heard. It catches me
mid-step. A tremor rises under my ribs; my throat locks. No
tears. No reason I can name.
Only this: the song is me.

I'm no light in anyone's life.
I don't matter to anyone—
just ashes scattered, already forgotten.
I'm not anyone's love,
not even anyone's enemy.

With no father as a model, a mother intent on domestication,
and boys who bully, my nervous system never builds the
pathways it needs to grow whole. Puberty's tide is approaching,
but my body isn't ready to carry it and braid it through my
cells.

Chapter 4

Age 12 ½

Saturday afternoon. Light pours lazy through the curtains. We sit in the family room with tea—delicate floral cups on a carved table. A Persian rug glows red-gold under our feet. Huma, fresh from the salon, leans into a brocaded cushion. Ashi hunches over her books on the floor. I half-watch from the sofa's edge.

Huma studies her nails, purple and new. "Ashi, you're seventeen. Time to start caring how you look. You can't stay like this forever—soon, the matchmakers will be at our door."

Ashi doesn't look up. Stray hair crosses her brow; homework walls her in. "I don't want a life where I'm a slave to a man. I'm going to work."

Huma's eyes flash. "Work? It isn't safe. Bosses, coworkers—they take advantage of women."

Ashi lifts her head, voice steady. "I know. One respectable path: doctor. Safe. Honorable."

Huma scoffs, shaking her head. "Medical school? Almost impossible. Too competitive."

Ashi underlines a sentence, closes the notebook. "That's why I work so hard."

Ashi sighs, then glances at me with a crooked grin before turning to Huma. "I'm sure he won't have to work—he'll inherit everything anyway."

Huma rolls her eyes. "I wish I were as special."

Just then, the phone shrills—five quick pulses, the code for an overseas call.
Mother and Father rush from their bedroom. Mother lifts the receiver; the rest of us hover barefoot around her.

A child's wail slides down the wire, then Nimra's panicked voice:
"He hit me again. The babies are crying ..."

Static swallows the rest. Mother's knuckles go white on the receiver.
Father leans in, jaw clenched, silent.
Huma sets her teacup on its saucer with surgical care; Ashi holds her breath.

Click. Line dead.
Ceiling fan ticks twice.

Father clears his throat. "We will pray for our daughter. It is sad, but it happens."
The room agrees by staying quiet.

Weeks after Nimra's call from America, the elders drift into our courtyard—Uncle Jamal first, smelling of motor oil and fennel; Aunt Shazia with her bangles in full jangle; Aunt Fozia, her sari pleats crisp enough to slice paper. Huma sits beside me in silence, while Ashi gathers her books and slips off to her room to study.

Mother pours tea. Father, shining in his starched collar, motions for me to shut the louvers to keep the heat out.
I reach up—sleeves suddenly short, fabric tugging at my shoulders. Shazia's gaze skims the fresh hair on my wrists but slides away.

"I wouldn't say a word if Huma were a boy. Men marry late without fuss—thirty, forty," Jamal says, dropping sugar into his cup. "But Huma is already twenty-two. In Pakistan, girls are married off by twenty."

Huma's chin dips. She doesn't argue, doesn't protest. She lowers her eyes and smooths the fabric over her knees, as if the cloth demands more attention than the words in the air. A girl bred to accept her fate absorbs talk like this without reply; silence is her good manners.

"Any later," Shazia adds, "and people will think something's wrong with her."
Father's mouth hardens with conviction. "Good families want brides at nineteen, twenty. An older daughter-in-law is hard to bend."

Everyone nods.

Mother blows on her tea. "You know I've been trying. I've turned down proposals, waiting for the right match—so Huma wouldn't end up like Nimra. She must like the man."

Huma raises her head, voice careful but steady. "Yes—please. Let me meet him before you decide. I don't want what happened to Nimra."

Fozia taps Shazia's elbow, tilting her head toward me. "He's shooting up like sugarcane."
Father waves it off. "Let him grow. We're talking about Huma."

Shazia says. "Every month Huma waits, the offers shrivel."

Huma's knuckles whiten, but she stays silent. The ceiling fan thuds overhead, stirring ginger-sweet air gone stale.

Mother sighs. "I'll find a new matchmaker. Someone fast."

I swallow—collar scraping my neck, the fabric already too small.

———————————

Rows of boys—white shirts, gray trousers—stand like fence posts in the assembly yard.
Beyond the wall, a diesel hum and a lone crow cries in the heat.
Behind me: breath, snicker, sting.
"Gorilla arms."
"Look—fur on his hands."
I keep still, arms welded to my sides. Hair I never voted for glints under the light. My voice, if it tries to answer, cracks itself in half.

Night. 00:43.
Snap awake—heart sprinting, skin swampy.
Sheet back: damp crescent spreading.
Bathroom light stutters on. Cold tile, colder terror. Dettol
antiseptic sting in the air.

Pajamas peeled, stain rinsed, soap scrubbed.
What sickness bleeds clear?
Wrung fabric, wet thighs, silent shuffle to bed.
Prayer: *Stop. Please stop.*

It doesn't. Three nights that week, then four—shame engulfs
me.

Morning ritual: heels to wall, pencil mark, check again
tomorrow.
Line always higher—taller than Father, than uncles.

Family weekend. Formal lounge full of Father's friends.
A hand jostles my hair—"Too tall for twelve."
Another voice. "Cut a hole in the roof for him."
Laughter shakes the chandelier.
Father slaps my back. "Enough—stop now."

Smile. Knees bend. Shoulders fold.

Puberty arrives like an occupying army—unannounced,
merciless. There is no warning—no sex-education class, no
whispered cousin-talk, no parent's quiet briefing. Five foot
nine—tallest in the class. Puberty hits before the rest.

A rumor arrives first: a ghazal singer has bought the house two lanes over—the one with the tall masonry wall and the dry fountain.

Soon her daughter, Mili, drifts into our courtyard, swapping recipes with my sisters. She is twenty, hair loose, laugh looser. Neighbors whisper about missing fathers and secret patrons, but the gossip slides off her like water off brass.

One afternoon I wrestle with an English composition; pages blur. Mili leans over the table.

"Subject, verb, object," she says, a pink-lacquered nail tapping the paper. "English is only math in disguise."

She offers to tutor me. Mother—thrilled—agrees.

Three days later, bicycle at my side, I ring their gate bell. The intercom crackles. A servant unlatches the gate. Palm fronds lift like green pennants. Stone pavers float across a koi pond, fountains arching glassy hoops.

Mili's mother opens the teak door. The voice I know from TV fills the porch—low, honeyed Urdu without a grain of Punjabi gravel.

Inside: marble coolness, mirror-worked cushions, dancers poised in gilt frames. A modern pulse threads through antique carvings.

On the patio, Mili spreads my notebook between us. Lessons become twice a week. Each day ends the same way: my bicycle ticking on its kickstand, Mili eyeing it like a dare.

"Let me sit?" she asks at last.
"Of course."

She perches sideways on the bike's top bar—a common way to ride as passengers in South Asia—ankles pressed together, toes pointed down, hands resting lightly on the handlebar. I hold the grips, my arms bracketing her so closely that they brush her shoulders with every turn. When the road bucks over a rut, her back touches my chest for a breath before she straightens.

My face goes hot, and my chest feels jumpy, like it can't decide what to do. I hold the handlebar tighter and stare at the road, counting cracks to steady myself. In, out. But the soft smell of her hair slips over to me and won't leave. I tighten my shoulders, trying to shrink into myself, trying to grasp the new, fluttery feeling that has no name yet.

Beyond the last houses, the road unspools through wheat stubble and sky. Mili sings a Noor Jehan melody—soft, steady, meant for wandering.

Thunder murmurs beyond the canal. I brake; we slide off the bicycle. A gray wall of cloud advances, slow and certain, the air thick with petrichor. We lie back on the warm earth—just as the first heavy drops strike our faces.

Then the monsoon arrives—sheets of rain so sudden they erase horizon, road, thought.
Clothes plaster, hair streaming, we laugh like children when adults aren't looking: astonished by how light the body can feel.

Something coiled inside me snaps open—fast, bright, terrifying. I let the water take me, let the sky answer back with thunder, let the ground become a drum.

When the curtain finally thins, we stand, mud-spattered and giddy. The bicycle gleams, droplets jeweling its scarlet paint.

Mili wrings her scarf-like *dupatta*, grins. "Same time Thursday?"
I nod—the only answer my body, suddenly and mercifully alive, can give.

Chapter 5

Late-night chill settles over the girls' room like a thin veil of frost. Huma sits cross-legged on the bed, fingers twisting a loose thread near her ankle.

"I wish our parents didn't treat me like freight," she mutters. "I swear I'll marry the next man who likes me—whoever he might be. It can't be worse than this house."

Her voice cracks. She stares at the wardrobe mirror but speaks to no one. Ashi, hunched over biology notes on the floor, looks up.

"They've tried ten times," Huma says, squaring her shoulders as if bracing for impact. "Ten rejections. Do you know what that feels like?"

Ashi's pencil pauses; silence answers for her.

Next Evening.
Ashi's textbooks stack like bricks on the study table. Huma sweeps past, eyes sharp.

"You really think grades will save you?" She flicks an index card to the floor. "Too ugly, too brainy—no one marries girls like you."

Ashi stoops, gathers the card, and slides it back into place. Her breath snags but holds. I watch from the doorway, a witness pinned to the frame.

Later, after lights out, I hear Ashi's muffled crying. I sit beside her, awkward arms around shaking shoulders, the way one props a branch so it won't snap under fruit. She cries; I don't. My own well is sealed, but her grief softens the dry earth around it.

Mother announces, "Guests on Saturday. The proposal is for an MD in Houston, Texas, thirty-two years old."

Saturday, 4 p.m.
A sharp knock. The MD's mother—hijab pinned, gaze hawklike—and his younger brother, Asif, all Western polish, walk in without the MD himself.
The formal lounge bristles with walnut and maroon upholstery. A crystal chandelier scatters small suns across the marble floor. The visitors' eyes sweep the room—calculation disguised as admiration.

Father greets them in fluent Punjabi, his rural warmth dialed high.

Huma enters with the tea tray, eyes lowered, steps small.
In a proposal visit, that is respect; direct eye contact would read as bold—a fault in a girl. The mother and brother's eyes move over her—posture, skin, wrists, even the way she places

the cups—each detail appraised. Her discomfort shows in the careful quiet of her hands, each movement too measured. In such rooms, the girl is expected to be a soft outline: pleasant, modest, pliable.

"My son waited until he was financially secure before seeking marriage," MD's mother says, placing a framed photo on the table: her son beside a Mercedes, a suburban house behind. The photo circles around the room. Huma lingers a breath; a subtle smile lifts, then fades.

The mother continues, "My son trusts me to choose his wife. He does not need to meet the girl. I already sent him the photographs the matchmaker showed me—he likes how Huma looks."

The room does not stir; to them, this is normal.

MD's mother turns to Huma. "Do you respect elders?"
"Yes, Auntie."
"Can you cook? Keep a house?"
"Yes, Auntie. I have a BA in Home Economics from a girls' college."
"You understand—you marry the family, not just the boy?"
Huma gives a final nod.

Asif fills the pauses with easy compliments, his smile calibrated for maximum charm. His watch flashes with every gesture, the gleam less about time than display.

Tea cools. The cuckoo clock chirps five.
The verdict begins to set like wet cement.

On the veranda, Father whispers, "Well?"
"Better than nothing," Mother murmurs, eyes on the departing hijab.

Huma's *yes* arrives by phone three weeks later, brief and final as a stamp: the doctor in Texas formally accepts. The wedding is penciled for late May—four months to turn a daughter into freight.

The engagement ceremony takes place without the groom. A photographer flashes bulbs in the lounge; Huma poses beside her future mother-in-law, who cradles a framed photo of her son like a remote control pointed at our future. Relatives applaud—doctor, dollars, destiny—and drift into the evening.

A week later.
The brass knocker barely settles before the front door swings open and Asif fills the frame. Twenty-nine, a successful engineer at a well-known multinational corporation, he lives in Taxila—seven hours from Lahore—with his mother. Single, he's next in line to be married.
He brings imported sweets balanced like treasure on one palm.

"Kids first," he says, winking. A Toblerone the length of my forearm lands in my hands, a board game in Ashi's, rose-pink bangles in Huma's. Laughter shakes loose from the walls in a way it never does when Father is home.
That night, we call him Brother Asif. He grins like a man slipping into a perfectly tailored coat.

"Can I take the kids to a movie?" he asks. Mother nods.

After the credits, he steers us to Liberty Market for fries dusted with chaat masala. On a concrete bench, he says, "Your father told me you're really good at math."
I nod, eyes still lowered.

"What other subjects do you like?" he continues.
"Physics."
"Wow, that's one of the tougher ones." He pats my back.
"And what don't you like?"
"History."

His attention is all on me. Every question, every smile—just for me. Father never treats me like that. No one does. For the first time, I feel truly noticed.

One day, when I come home from school, shoulders tight, eyes burning from another day of jeers and shoves, he's already in the living room.
"Hey, you okay?" he asks.
I stare at the floor, unable to answer. His hand rests gently on my back—warm, steady. I don't know how much I long for that kind of touch until it lands.
Mother's voice cuts in from the kitchen: "Lunch is ready." We all sit down together at the table, plates passing, voices low, while the warmth of his hand lingers inside me.

Asif begins visiting more, as work often brings him to Lahore. My parents welcome him each time. For them, every visit is reassurance for Huma: close in-law ties mean the engagement will hold. In Pakistan, parents hesitate to propose marriage for girls with broken engagements. Widows and divorcees bear an even heavier stigma.

During his next visit.
Heat presses against the windows, but the living room stays museum-cool beneath the AC. I curl into the ragged sofa corner, reading *Tintin*.

A sharp knock.
Mother calls: "Faraz, door!"

I pad across marble that numbs my soles. Asif stands there—shirt crisp, grin sharper—arms stacked with three bright LEGO boxes: Galaxy Explorer, Yellow Castle, Technic Super Car.

"Champ!" He edges inside, piling the treasure at my feet. "I thought we could play together."

Something opens under my ribs, warm and surprising, like a tree waking up after winter. Asif ruffles my hair—gentle this time—and lets his hand stay on my neck.

He slices open the space set first, gray and blue bricks skittering over the glass table. As we snap fuselage plates together, his thigh presses lightly against mine—steady, deliberate. My body drinks the contact like cracked earth drinking the first rain.

Huma passes through, drying her hands on an apron, and mouths, "So sweet," before vanishing into clattering dishes.

By dusk, the starship stands complete, its yellow canopy catching the last light. Asif taps the cockpit. "Captain's chair—yours."

A laugh escapes—unpracticed, bright. He echoes it, eyes holding mine a heartbeat too long before squeezing my shoulder, firm, approving.

Long after his car growls away, I sit on the floor, ship resting on my knees, scalp tingling where his fingers have been. The house feels newly spacious, as if its rooms have stretched like branches to catch fresh light, a story growing brick by brick, promise by promise—balanced on the trembling keel of being chosen.

He begins staying overnight whenever he visits Lahore. Though the guest room is empty, Mother tells him to sleep in mine. We share the double bed beneath the steady fan. At night he hugs me before I drift off, and I hug him back. For a boy starved of a father's attention, that warmth feels like a safety I've never known. With each visit, the hugs return, as familiar as the fan's hum. Nothing more—just the hugs.

Like my parents and like Nimra, Huma meets her husband for the first time on the wedding day. In Pakistan, sex is expected that night, though most girls arrive in that bed knowing nothing about it. Nine months later, she delivers her first child. After the wedding, Mother asks Huma if her husband likes her, but she does not ask whether Huma likes him.

Huma's visa papers stall, her husband flies back to Houston the same week, and Huma returns to our house to wait.

In Pakistan, husbands and in-laws are expected to care for the bride. When summer arrives, my parents send Huma and me to stay at the in-laws' house, asking me to keep her company.

43

The in-laws' house has three bedrooms and a lounge with oversized couches. Huma takes the only free bedroom; the other two belong to her mother-in-law and to Asif.

Asif nudges my elbow. "You'll bunk with me. Natural, isn't it?" Huma stacks bangles on a dresser, not looking up. "Yes. Obviously."
Asif sets his suitcase by the bed. Pats the mattress—inviting, certain.

The window frames a ficus tree trembling in evening wind. I step inside, duffel still on my shoulder. The door eases shut behind me.

Chapter 6

Ages 13 to 16

The latch settles with a courteous click, and night seeps through the window like dye through water.

The silence is so complete I hear my own pulse ticking in my ears—a nervous clock with no hands.

I lay on the far edge of the double bed, knees to chest, rehearsing the slow breath Mother called *good manners*.

The mattress dips, a faint rustle of cloth, his weight aligning behind me—like a second shadow at noon.

First slide of his hand.
Hesitates at the elastic—then inside.
Only one thought: Nowhere to run.
Second thought jams, choking.
Limbs: lead.
Pressure. Splitting. Bones hold; the rest shatters.

I exit the body, leave it cooling on the bed.
Up—into the dark ceiling.
Time buckles.
Watching.
Nothing left to feel.

When he guides my hand to him, the ceiling-self drifts farther, scatters like sparks from a welding torch. The room glows blue for an instant, then black again.
He finishes, rolls away.
The ceiling fan whirrs its lazy blades, counting the seconds until the world pretends nothing has happened.

A boy drifts through a shapeless sky, searching for a star bright enough to name what he lost.

That summer at Asif's, he takes me to his office with a light hand on my shoulder, steering me through doorways. "He's a brilliant student—poised for success," he tells colleagues, chin lifting, palm warm between my shoulder blades—pride my father never voices. He lets me spin in his chair, ruffles my hair, and grins. We go shopping; he matches my pace, looks over the bicycle frames with me, asks what I think and listens. In the park he sends the frisbee high just to watch me run, clapping when I catch it. In the evenings he takes us out—his mother, Huma, and me. He seats me next to him, asks what I want, and then orders for me.

Nights are a different story. After the lights go out, hugs give way to him masturbating me, and then he makes me masturbate him—same as the first time. Later, he starts kissing me too. We never speak of the nights; I somehow know it must stay secret. My nervous system splits to survive: by day I soak in his father-warmth; by night I dissociate from my body.

When school resumes, Huma is in Texas, but Asif still returns—sometimes monthly, sometimes twice a week. Mother keeps putting him in my room, never once asking how I feel or what happens when the lights go out. Father's jaw tightens at his visits. He avoids him but never asks me anything. Asif replays the same routine—no escalation. The visits stop after two years, when he has his arranged marriage.

———————————

In the first weeks of that summer at his house, I stay deeply dissociated during the assaults. I feel nothing until ejaculation. Only later does sensation return, but it's limited to sexual pleasure and the feeling of skin on skin. My limbs and the rest of my body remain absent; everything beyond that narrow circuit is blank.

I have seen nothing erotic—no photographs, no glossy magazines, no films—and I haven't touched myself before he does. I should have been inside my body—feeling muscle thicken, testosterone rise, letting myself enjoy the becoming of these years. Instead, arousal comes only through closeness with an adult man, while the rest of me stays numb. The pattern sets in early—arousal without embodiment, pleasure without feeling my muscles—etches itself into my nervous system when I should be learning to enjoy my body, to explore desire on my own terms.

My upbringing makes me deeply susceptible to men like Asif. He exploits the father hunger I carry; I lean toward him instinctively, hoping he might fill that gap. The anger that should have defended me never reaches my brain or muscles. It stays trapped somewhere deeper, so I can't think or move against what is happening. My body, once trained to play a role in my parents' marriage drama, now fawns to play the role he wants.

I later learned the name for what fastened me to him: a trauma bond.

The long-term abuse often follows a cycle: moments of harm—fear, pain, or humiliation—are interrupted by periods of kindness, apology, or affection. This creates reinforcement, which trains the brain to associate the abuser with both danger and safety. Love and fear get tangled together.

Over time, this conditioning can create loyalty, affection, and even dependence on the person causing harm. As a child, I didn't realize the abuse was wrong. It felt like survival: if the *father* figure sometimes offered comfort, protection, or rewards, my nervous system clung to those moments as a lifeline. Compared to my parents' treatment, it even felt better. Leaving wasn't just difficult—it seemed impossible, because the thought of it filled me with loneliness and the fear of abandoning the only warmth and sexual pleasure I knew.

Later I learned the cruel twist: the brain does not distinguish between safe touch and unsafe touch when releasing bonding chemicals. During assault, oxytocin—the same hormone that normally fosters love and trust—can surge. This creates feelings of closeness to the very person causing harm. That is why trauma bonds are often called betrayal bonds: the body's natural chemistry is being hijacked in a dangerous context.

At the same time, ongoing abuse keeps cortisol—the stress hormone—chronically elevated. High cortisol damages the hippocampus, the brain's memory and context center. This makes it harder to see patterns of harm clearly, leaving a person foggy, doubting their own perceptions, and more dependent on the abuser's version of reality.

The Split

1983

Chapter 7

Ages 16 to 20

Even so, puberty moves through—crooked, intent.

I tackle the ball with my foot, strike it clean, and it rockets past the keeper, snapping the net. One stunned heartbeat; dust hangs in the late light. Then the field explodes. The cheer slams into my chest. Teammates swarm—palms drumming my back, someone ruffling my hair, my name chanted like a beat. We jump, we laugh, we collapse into a ridiculous, glowing pile—grass on my knees, sweat-salt in my mouth, breath all light. For once my body says yes. Not outside. We are us—and I'm inside it. I belong.

My sixteenth birthday arrives riding the high of that winning goal. The same boys who'd once tripped me now smear frosting across my cheek. They laugh loud and easy in our living room. For a moment, my life feels rebuilt, laughter filling in the cracks.

I build my new self on that laughter and frosting—6'2", good looks, grades, easy confidence. I play the part so well I convince everyone—most days, even myself—that the confidence runs marrow-deep.

Then I go to the gym with friends.
One loses his grip; a dumbbell crashes onto another boy's foot.
The boy howls, clutching his toes. My friend stammers an
apology, hand out to help—but the injured boy jerks away,
face reddening, and shoves him hard. Voices spike. My friend
shoves back, harder.

Metal clatters. Benches scrape.

The two boys square off, eyes lit with rage, chests puffing. My
friends close in fast—arms out, voices snapping—forming a wall
to hold the fight back.

I don't move. Terror roots me. Heart pounding, breath ragged,
a hot ache throbs in my lower back with every pulse. I stay
frozen, watching them hold their ground while my body curls
inward, trembling.

The fight dissolves. We lift again.
Their reps ring true; mine feel hollow, out of tune.
My gut holds an absolute truth. I can't sense my muscles from
the inside the way they do—I barely feel what's within.

They have something I don't. A fault line under the new life
begins to grind. I dare not go near; I tiptoe around it.

My body is tall, lean, and thin—but that isn't the wound. I don't
lack size; I lack power—never taught to protect myself, trained
instead to stay small and disappear. Why would I build muscle
for a life spent hiding?

———————————————

After elementary school, boys and girls our age aren't allowed to be alone together. Most schools enforce strict separation; only a few colleges mix the sexes. I go to an all-boys school.

Outside of school, the only interaction with marriage-eligible girls is in affluent liberal homes like mine, or with cousins—cousin marriage is common, even expected. I never feel that pull toward my cousins. All boy–girl contact is closely policed, and pre-marital sex is considered a sin.

With no public language for homosexuality, desire between boys isn't named—so, with no girls their age around to experiment with and hormones surging, many test desire with other boys, openly among friends, while still talking about girls.

For me, anything sexual feels dangerous. I don't talk, and I don't experiment; I keep quiet or slip away.

In secret, Asif-shaped fantasies keep replaying. That's the only way I can arouse myself. Pleasure feels prewritten by ancient geology. His looks repulse me, but the fantasies aren't mine to choose.

Sixteen bleeds into eighteen in one long, low-rumbling aftershock.

Ashi misses the medical college cut-off by less than a percent. For a week, she stays shut in her room—barely eating, hardly speaking, no tears. When she emerges, something has gone still: footsteps muted, plates set down without a clink.

The matchmaker circles soon after. Things move quickly: a handful of visits, a tidy list of virtues. Stamped. Approved.

One afternoon, the groom comes to the formal lounge. She sits with him for only a few minutes—just the two of them—and they like each other. He's an established mechanical engineer living in Lahore. The wedding soon follows.

But Ashi's story doesn't end in that silence. She later earns a master's in Botany, cultivates a garden that overflows with color, and builds a small landscaping business on the side.

———————

The physics lab smells of hot wires and chalk dust. Mr. Hameed taps my final exam gently. "Ninety-eight point six—top half-percent again, Faraz." His rare smile softens even the harsh glare of ceiling lights. Classmates pat my shoulder; someone jokes I have hidden batteries powering my brain. For a moment, happiness floods me—I belong.

In Pakistan, college students don't work until after graduation—unemployment is so high that even odd jobs are scarce. My evenings go unclaimed. I slip into the American Center, the British Council, the Alliance Française—films, journals, lectures; rooms where ideas breathe without clerics at the door. The promise is simple: think freely, no script. I feel the pull of an untethered life.

One afternoon in the months following my high school graduation, I cycle home along Canal Road, eucalyptus trees tall and fragrant overhead. Mother waits at the gate, holding a cream envelope stamped with the college crest my father reveres. On the porch, I slit it open: an acceptance letter, embossed motto, *University of Engineering and Technology*—words shimmering with promise.

University gates open to new terrain: girls debating calculus over chai; dorm corridors buzz past midnight; a courtyard where guitar strings compete with the muezzin's call. One evening, a classmate named Afia brushes my elbow as she passes the sugar; my forearm tingles—sunlight pours through my veins. No jolt of dread, no ice cracking—just aliveness.

Saturday nights belong to the tea stall outside Hostel 3. Ten of us—boys and girls—circle dented kettles, steam rising softly into the dark. Someone cracks a joke, and laughter fills the air, loosening my shoulders, warmth settling deep in my bones. Moments like these make the campus feel like home.

The ground holds—despite deep fissures rumbling below—until the day I turn twenty.

Confidence climbs: new campus, new muscles, a lane in the pool that feels like private airspace. Coach Malik's hand on my scapula adjusts a stroke here, a kick there, guiding me forward each week.

A month later.

Dusk—
I sit on my bed, calculus notes in my lap.
The ground gives way.
A fissure yawns.

My notebook skids across the floor.
Tears detonate: full-bodied, unstoppable.
Gravity drags me into the gap. Free fall—a bottomless plunge.
The void swallows me whole.
Then the plates slam shut.

Malik's face floods in—chlorine-bleached hair, whistle cord,
steady eyes—no longer a coach but a magnet. I find him
repulsive. Asif scenes splice into Malik frames, the projector
jams in a loop.
I hate the film, yet I can't leave the theater.
I masturbate.

Days blur; food tastes like cardboard. Friends' jokes crackle like
distant radio static.

The Malik fantasies keep screening, painful and uncut, every
single day. I stop swimming so I don't have to see him.

As if that reel weren't punishment enough, terror seizes every
moment. On the road, I twist toward the rearview mirror
at every turn—knuckles white, sweat beading—convinced a
phantom car hugs my tail, closing in with each blink of its
headlights.

At night, I wake every hour, lungs seizing against the dark,
stumble to grip the bedroom knob—still latched, still not
enough—while my heart pounds for minutes before I can lie
down again.

Above it all, I climb to the university rooftop most afternoons,
the wind hissing like a dare; I stare into the chasm below, half

longing for free fall, half paralyzed by the terror that even this escape might fail me.

I give friends only scraps—a muttered mention of sleepless nights, the way I check every door twice—but never the abuse itself. Then I scrounge loose bills for a therapist—to help me figure out if I am gay.

Malik is ten years older, an authority figure. Something about the intimacy in the pool—just swimming trunks, sometimes a little apart in the corner of the Olympic-size pool, often at night—stirs my body's memory of Asif. My body had fused arousal with Asif—and now with him—despite his repulsiveness. The hypervigilance and dread that seize me are the feelings I couldn't feel with Asif.

Chapter 8

Ages 20 to 22

My therapist's appointment is only days away when it happens.

Gates clang, and my parents' friends, who've recently moved to Lahore, drift indoors trailing whispers of spice and incense. Among them is their daughter, Samira, jasmine-quiet, eyes the mellow brown of steeped tea. The formal lounge fissures along its usual seams—men orbiting politics, women trading rumor—so I invite her to the family room, a gesture rehearsed yet suddenly sincere.

We begin with the surface facts: she is studying English Literature; I, Electrical Engineering. Then I ask, "What do you like to do?"

She tilts her head, considering. "I write poems no one sees. I read them once, then fold them away. And I listen to songs my parents call vulgar."

I am fascinated. I have never met a woman like that before—different, unapologetic, carrying secret words and forbidden music. Until now, women in my world have been defined by what they are allowed; she speaks as if she can define herself.

Her voice spills into names—Abida Parveen, vast and unbroken; Bob Dylan, restless and insistent. I light up at the overlap, songs we both carry like secret keepsakes. We both stand outside the religious script. Conversation loops between music, childhood memories, and pauses that feel more alive than words.

Mystery curls at the edges of the room, as if something more wants to be spoken but chooses, instead, to remain unsaid.

Three evenings later, the landline rings.
"Meet again?"

Dusk finds us in an empty market lot, the red Corolla ticking as it cools in amber light. I slip inside and pull the door shut.

Removing her sunglasses, she smiles. "I've been replaying those moments."
"Same reel over here," I admit.

I feel the slow thrum of blood under my skin, breath uncoiling, vision pin-sharp—as if I've just stepped into my body for the first time. Heat climbs my neck; she is blushing too. Our eyes hold—both of us wanting to glance away, yet unable. Something unfamiliar blooms inside me; I can't name it, only know it is precious.

Words finally catch up. We confess we like each other—and then meet the social clock: I am twenty; she is nineteen. Our world presses her toward marriage; I am still a dependent, not ready. She sighs, almost under her breath, "If only I weren't bound by their clock." The truth hovers like a posted warning. Still, we choose to continue.

Later that evening, I stand naked before the mirror—spring's first sapling, tender yet sure in the soil. Every sensation sharpens: muscle stretching like new bark, breath lifting and falling effortlessly. For the first time, my body is my home—windows open, warmth spilling outward. My palm finds my sternum; beneath it, the quiet animal pulses. In that glow, I know: I belong to myself, entirely.

The Malik reel that has looped for months stops cold; the fantasies vanish in a single breath. I cancel the therapist's appointment. I can't name what I feel about Malik, only that I am not gay.

The telephone becomes an artery. From midnight to dawn, we pour ourselves through it—confessing not only our longing but also the heat of it. We describe, in detail, what we wish to do to each other, tracing desires that leave us flushed and trembling, until words themselves feel like touch.

A week later.
In the courtyard, bougainvillea blazes scarlet in the noon heat. Our knees brush; Samira leans in gently—I rise to meet her. Lips touch, warm and certain. Her palm rests above my heart, my hand tracing the promise of her spine. The world stills, as if the courtyard itself holds its breath.

A month later.
Her window slides open and moonlight spills silver across the jasmine vines. She draws me in—both of us barefoot—as the door clicks shut. Clothes slide off in a rush; skin recognizes skin.

For a moment I freeze. But Samira reaches first, her voice whispering what she wants, with a tenderness I have never known. No secrecy. No fear.

My body unshackles, unafraid. Heat gathers wild, the last space closes, and the night keeps our secret.

What began in shadow spills into daylight—cafés, markets, long drives.

We tuck into a café corner, voices and steam hissing us into a small cocoon. Samira leans back, laughing at her own line. The door opens; a man walks in—tall, muscular, athletic.

My legs fade. Air thickens. I stare at the cup.

The same old truth moves in my bones: I cannot feel muscles the way he does.
I feel less than him, less of a man.

Under the table, my palm finds Samira's thigh—warm, solid. She covers my hand with hers. My ribs loosen; my jaw unlatches. The man fades from my mind.

Numbness lets go; feeling runs down my legs like water into dry soil.

Samira squeezes my hand and asks, "Everything okay?"
I smile, nod. She keeps talking, eyes bright, hands alive.

Driving home, I take stock of what my body knows. Imagining Malik was arousal braided with dread—a private horror reel. The man in the café triggered the same splice. With Samira, my body remains sure. Her softness yields to my strength; my muscles thicken, pulse steady. No tremors, no hesitation—just clarity, proof I've found my ground.

Since we'd been together, the old fantasies had gone quiet. Next to what I feel with her, they read as injury, not desire. I love Samira and want her. If I were truly gay, I tell myself, I would feel it with friends too.

I never tell her about Asif or Malik. Deep down, I fear she'll get scared of the broken parts of me—just like I am—and turn away. At the time, I don't even have the words for it myself—couldn't have told her, even if I'd tried.

Weeks pass before Mother and Father call me into their room. In Lahore, being seen in public with someone not her brother marks a girl; rumor travels faster than cars.
"Sit," Father says, voice flat, serious.
I lower myself onto the edge of the bed. The curtains are half-drawn; the room smells of stale perfume.

Father begins. "Samira's father came to me. He said you've been seeing each other—a friend saw you together in a restaurant."

Mother's eyes flood. "I am ashamed of you. You're ruining our reputation. Did I bring you into this world to face public humiliation?"

"Is it true?" Father asks. "Are you two seeing each other? Do you like her?"
My throat tightens; silence holds me for a beat. Then I nod.

Father presses on. "And now her father—one of my oldest friends—is concerned. Word has spread, and in people's eyes Samira is spoken of as loose."

The talk ends. Within the hour, the phone rings. Samira. Her voice is shredded. She tells me her parents said worse—spat the word every girl fears but no one says aloud. She begs, "Marry me." My mind blanks. "I don't earn, not ready yet." I say, the only truth I can reach, and end the call.

The next day, my parents come to my room. They say they've spoken with Samira's parents and decided to get us engaged—not for our love, but to shield both families' reputations.
"What about America—for my master's?" I ask.
"We'll marry you when you return," they say. "You still have a year before you leave."

I am elated.

With Samira, I feel the full spectrum—laughter, quarrels, and touch. She's quick and exacting, challenges me, calls my shit out. Sometimes she raises her voice, then shows me how anger can burn clean and pass. "Our love can hold everything," she often whispers, her lips brushing mine.

We drive fast, racing each other along the empty roads outside Lahore, wind in our faces; we can talk for hours and never find the bottom. And yes—our touch makes us gentler, truer.

But even in that joy, caution presses close. I still waver around certain men, though with Samira my sexuality holds steady, a lifeline. Her company keeps the worst fantasies far from shore.

I don't want to think about any of that—being with her is enough.

An hour later I am at her gate. I ring, then knock, then ring again. When Samira opens the door I blurt it all at once—"Congratulations"—and wrap her in a hug, kissing her cheek, the apology tumbling out for how curt I've been on the phone. She goes stiff, eyes flashing. "Idiot," she says, giving my chest a quick, angry thump—and then she pulls me in and holds on, hard, the anger dissolving like mist in sunlight.

That summer, Huma and Nimra are visiting us from the States. Over afternoon tea, Nimra and Ashi, through tears, share how their husbands hurt them—with words and with blows; Huma thanks Allah that her marriage has only emotional abuse, before quietly admitting that she is afraid even one no might bring a slap.

The conversation continues.

Ashi asks, "How do you preserve family values in America—such a liberal country?"
Huma says, "We keep to our own. A small Pakistani circle, same mosque. After school, the children go there to read Quran and learn our values."
Nimra adds, "Yes. I'm proud of us—my community is the same."
Ashi presses gently, "Do you think your children will have

arranged marriages too?"
"We are trying our best," they answer together.

To me, their talk rings hollow. American films and afternoons
at the American Center, the British Council, and the Alliance
Française have already tutored me in other possibilities—the
power of individuality over conformity. My parents praise
Huma and Nimra for upholding family values as we rinse the
cups and lay out plates for the dinner we are hosting for Samira
and her family.

Food stretches warm and easy across the table—steam lifting
from pilaf, the clink of silverware, Nimra and Huma trading
jokes while Ashi steals the last kebab. My parents sit looser
than I've seen in years; Samira's mother keeps pressing more
lentils into everyone's bowls, her father laughing at his own
one-liners. Samira's brother teases her about the way she's
arranged the salad, and she flicks him a look that promises later
revenge.

After dessert, Ashi grins. "Samira, sing." In our families,
someone is always coaxed into a song after the plates are
cleared. She waves it off, then her mouth curves and she nods.
"Just a little," she says.

Her voice slips into the air—soft at first, a love song barely
above the porcelain hush. When our eyes meet, she laughs,
color bright in her cheeks, and hides behind her hand.
"I can't—not while he's looking at me," she says, glowing. She
turns to the window, draws a breath, and begins again.

This time her voice blooms like jasmine at dusk—sweet,
certain, and full. Conversation falls away; the room holds still.

I sit, lit from within—my body steady, a fortress—as the woman I love sings to the room, feeling this way among my own family for the first time in my life.

We see no reason to hide our love after the engagement. We move between our homes like a tide—tea at hers, dinner at mine—palms linked in front of our parents. The rulebook loosens—courage strikes, setting tinder alight. We are deliriously in love and it shows—doorway grins, kitchen whispers—as if a cinema romance has slipped its frame and settled into our kitchens and living rooms.

We forget that in Pakistan, romance is a film, not a family scene.

My sisters' whispers begin to shift the air.
"He's too happy with her."
"Has anyone seen him so happy before?"
"She's clever."
"She'll snatch him from all of us."
"And who is going to take care of you in your old age?"
"She's lewd. No decent girl behaves like that with her fiancé."
"She's destroying our family's honor."

They play on the deepest fears of Pakistani parents, until my parents' worry grows wild. I hold fast to Samira—more visits, fingers laced in plain sight—but by the time Nimra and Huma fly back to the States, my parents embrace their darkest side. They curse her in daylight, call her love a performance, a trap, and ask me to leave her.

My parents' wishes pluck the old strings, and the child inside me performs like a puppet. It feels as though my life belongs to them, not to me. I drift in a fog, bewildered and powerless. I don't protest; instead, I sink into depression. Still, I cling to one small act of defiance: I refuse to remove my ring and ask her to keep hers on as well.

When my parents take their disapproval to her family, the strain begins to wear her down—our laughter thins; our dates go taut with silence. Samira fears not only losing us but being married into a life she doesn't want. Her pleas sharpen: "Marry me now—don't go to the USA."

Soon after, my parents put it plain: return the engagement ring to Samira's parents or the U.S. is off—no ticket, no tuition. I have no job to stand on, no income of my own.

Even then, I refuse.

My parents seize control, put a blade to our promise, and deliver the verdict to her parents.

I beg Samira to wait—just one more year. I promise I'll find a one-year master's program, start earning, and return for her, or find a way to bring her to America.
"Going to America is air to me," I try to explain.
She refuses. "My parents won't let me wait that long."

A week later, she tells me families are already arriving with matchmakers to evaluate her. The words shred whatever is left of my heart. Helpless, like a man clinging to the ground as it splits open beneath him.

Within three months, Samira is married off in an arranged match to a stranger—and she tells me not to contact her again.

A few weeks later.
Tight-lipped goodbyes.
Wheels lift. Lahore blurs to haze beneath.
Fault lines grind.

Only altitude.
Only hollowness.

New Ground

1989

Chapter 9

Ages 22 to 24

The jet's wheels kiss the runway, and passengers spill into concourses of glass and chrome, where even echoes seem pre-programmed. Footsteps slide in measured cadence, each pivot foretold by flawless English signs. The air—laundered, bleach-bright—refuses every diesel trace of Lahore. Beyond the windows, Atlanta unspools in eight-lane currents of asphalt curling around mirror-skinned towers; traffic glides as if the city's clocks tick beneath its roads.

Inside, I carry another country.
What Samira's laughter once held together, now rips apart.
Seams pry open—quiet at first, then sharp; edges salt-rimmed, sore.
I walk the Chattahoochee trails and let the river carry what I can't. Grief rises in tides: first a hush, then a current, then collapse, until I liquefy—an ocean poured into red clay, every drop received, every sorrow held.

I survive that first Georgia Tech quarter by immersing myself in coursework and leaning on the wilderness to steady me. In a dorm room tucked inside a shared apartment, I keep to myself. Professors mark my graphs with praise; classmates nod at my careful teamwork. On the surface, I appear polished, composed. Underneath, I am just holding on.

Second quarter, ten minutes before Advanced Calculus, a fellow student from Lahore, also here for his degree, comes up—handsome, with a bright, open smile. "Ismail," he says. We slide easily into friendship—study sessions that stretch past dusk, quick snacks after soccer, the kind of unforced conversation that leaves room for silence. His warmth and humor settle me, letting me feel not just welcome but wanted. Yet the very ease of his openness brushes an old bruise. I feel echoes of what I felt with Asif and Malik—too close, too familiar.

He catches me Friday morning after Applied Physics.
"Weekend plans?"
"Chattahoochee River hike—Saturday."
"Can I join?"
"Sure."
"Want to come to Friday prayers at the mosque?"
"No. I'm not religious."

Ismail blinks—surprised—but smooths it away.
"See you tomorrow morning."
"Looking forward to it."

The next sunny morning on the trail, we climb corkscrewing switchbacks, resin bleeding from the pines into the warm air. After some chatter, I tell him about Samira and her loss, my voice raw.

"I'm sorry," he says. "I will let my parents find me a wife. It is what a good son does."

The conversation thins to small talk. We take a snack break; he skims off his T-shirt, then shucks his joggers—bronze torso lacquered in sun, thighs braided like live-oak roots beneath blood-red shorts. His strength presses the same bruise—the ache of knowing he can feel and build his muscles, while I cannot.

By late afternoon we finish the hike. He slows beside me, shoulder brushing mine. When I turn, his eyes hold mine a beat too long; color rises in his cheeks. He pulls me into a quick, gentle hug, his hand resting warm on my shoulder. "I had a great time with you," he says softly. "Let's do this again soon."

I like resting in the hum of his muscles. Childhood cut me off from my own; abuse deepened the split. To cope, I borrow his maleness—enough to feel briefly complete.
Without my knowing, my body quietly compensates for stalled childhood development.

A couple of weeks later, the trail lies quiet in the late light. As the slope evens, he drifts closer until our elbows brush. The third time our arms touch, he lingers. Heat slips from his skin into mine. He doesn't look at me. I meet his eyes; his fingers tighten around mine. He tugs me in. His arm folds around me in a quick, unsure hug that lingers one beat past safe—too warm to be friendship.
I want to ask what's happening, but words don't form. My body moves as it did with Asif—silent, compliant, letting him decide.

That night hits hard: Ismail's sideways, unspoken wanting pulls me under, triggering the memory of Asif's grooming—and its aftermath.

Face jams into the pillow, salt leaks.
Room spins—sucked into the black hole Malik once opened.
Floor disappears.
I go with it.
I push a hand under the elastic and masturbate.

Memories of Ismail saturate my mind—no Malik or Asif. I feel only the sexual pleasure; the rest of my body stays absent, as it did with Asif.

Over the next weeks we meet often—study rooms, cheap dinners, evening walks—easy because he lives nearby in off-campus housing. The pattern holds: small touches, quick side hugs, the same quiet advances, never escalating.

I start finding reasons to pass his street, just to feel near him. When a day goes by without seeing him, something in me fidgets. In private, the fantasies keep running, automatic.

When the quarter ends, Ismail flies to Pakistan for the summer. I stay behind, stack extra courses, determined to finish early.

———————————

My family stays curt and distant. No one asks how I'm carrying Samira's loss. I offer grades and weather; they return advice and silence. I don't see Huma or Nimra in the States—Atlanta and their cities might as well be planets apart.

I make new friends—mostly Indian and American. The Indian students feel easy: shared food, shared jokes, no one policing my secular leanings. With most Pakistanis, I feel watched for a piety I don't have. The Americans fascinate me—a window I've only known through Hollywood now opens onto how they think and move through the world.

Most weekends I hike the woods and let the trees hold what I can't. I carry Samira's poems and photographs in my backpack, reading a line on a boulder and missing her unabashed boldness—how she lights up any room—and wondering how she's surviving the rip. She's a maverick in a world that trains girls to fold; I love her for that.

I miss the body I had with her—inhabited, lit from within; now it feels possessed, as if Asif still rides my nerves, trauma dulling my body-sense—the opposite of that bright, rooted presence with Samira.

Ismail enters that season like an echo. We share little: his views run with conservative Pakistan, mine run against the current. Anything beyond small talk gets clipped fast.

My attraction to Ismail is a complicated, powerful force. I carry a hollowness from my childhood, a sense of being fundamentally incomplete. I siphon his maleness to patch the holes in myself. His indirect invitations spark old wiring—arousal rising before I can stop it. Merging with him sexually feels like the body's ultimate answer—to touch the manhood I can't feel inside.

Before I can think, the fantasies are already running—a bridge my psyche builds to make sense of the pull. I remake the scene—this time with Ismail—handsome, a peer, my age. The fantasy softens the trauma into something I can bear, the way a child might redraw a frightening picture with a gentler monster.

I use the word maleness, not masculinity, because what I long for isn't a masculine image—it's the felt presence of manhood in my body.

———————————————

Fall quarter, Ismail returns. Second year clicks back into place; I'm six months from graduating, and my days orbit him like a bad habit. I call it friendship. It feels like thirst. I reroute walks past his off-campus unit, listen for his knock, scan the hallways between classes.

We keep the pattern: study rooms, cheap curries, long loops around the intramural fields. Now I start reaching first—an arm over his shoulder, fingers seeking his, a hand at his nape—and his face hardens, sudden winter. Warmth drains, eyes go flat, and I retreat, apology in my throat. For days I avoid his street, trying to will the hunger down. Then he returns as if nothing happened—soft-eyed, easy smile, palm grazing my back in a cafeteria line, a side hug a beat too long. The frost gone, the warmth back, we reset.

Each night the reel winds tighter. I promise to let the fantasies go; by midnight they have me again. Obsession gives my days a pulse: find him, read him, stay near. Despair shadows the same steps: he isn't mine; I'm not his; I don't even want to want this—and yet I do.

Then Ismail stops by—voice warm—inviting me into the mountains for an overnight camping trip, just the two of us. Out before dawn, back the next morning. I say yes.

The Great Smoky Mountains cradle us in early fall; we hike shirtless, bodies glinting, shoulders brushing now and then, fingers finding each other on the narrower bends as the breeze ripples through the trees.

That night on the ridge, embers pulse gently, heat tracing the edges of our silence. When it's time to turn in, we peel off our shirts before crawling into the tent—skin bare to the night, breath close in the dark. His leg brushes mine—warm, electric—and neither of us move away.

My breath catches; I reach for his hand, slow, trembling.
He squeezes back—firm. My fingers begin tracing the curves of his chest, slow, exploratory.
He freezes, then rolls away.

At dawn, we pack in silence.
Midway through the drive home, I break.
"I care about you—more than a friend. I thought you felt it too."
Eyes on the road, he answers flat: "I'm not interested."

I pull back just enough to look at him. "Then why the intimacy?" I ask, my voice low. "If this is only friendship, why hold my hand, why hug me like that?"

"You don't judge me. That makes you safe."
"Safe for what?"
Silence.

I sit quietly, tears streaking now and then.
At my door I tell him, "I can't keep seeing you the same way.
It's too painful."
He nods—unreadable.

Through graduation I keep things formal between us—never
alone together.

Afterward I anchor myself in Atlanta as a software engineer
at a major telecom—salary, benefits, security guaranteed. I
rent a spacious apartment in Northwest Atlanta, next to the
Chattahoochee River, where evening hikes feel like medicine.

Chapter 10

Age 24 to 25

Morning pours through the south-facing glass, bright enough to warm the desk. Downtown stacks in clean planes—mirrored facades, a slice of sky. The floor hums: badge beeps, elevator sighs, the soft percussion of keyboards. From the kitchen drifts a kaleidoscope of accents—Tamil, Spanish, Mandarin, Georgia drawl—swirled with the smell of coffee and bagels. I share a two-person office with Steve, his desk always neat. Our door opens into a lounge of couches and plants, skylights washing the wooden planks in daylight.

I write code in the sunlight. Greg, my manager, scopes it for four weeks, but I finish in two. He pauses at my desk and slides a sticky note onto my keyboard: *Impressive speed and accuracy—well done.* My chest loosens a notch.

Rina finds me at the coffee machine around three—arms loosely crossed, an unguarded smile, thin gold-rimmed glasses catching a glint from the window. A cotton top, an airy skirt, scuffed walking shoes—the opposite of performative.

"You're Faraz, right?" she says. "I market what you write. We'll be working together."

"Yes, good to meet you, Rina. I remember you from the meeting this morning."

We take our cups to the lounge. Conversation unfolds easily: her suburban Atlanta childhood, my Lahore alleys and love for nature. She's American, roughly my age, her parents originally from Gujarat, India. She asks if I'll join a lunch she's organizing to brainstorm new product ideas. I say yes.

Back at my desk, Steve asks, without looking up from his terminal,
"Weekend plans?"
"Hiking."
"Bicycling."
Bicycling! My legs hum, already spinning.

The office breathes around us—diverse, bright, alive. I keep my eyes on the code, let the rhythm hold.

A few weeks later. Fluorescents buzz. Cursor blinks. Sun warms the desk.
Tom, a peer, fills the doorway. "I went through your code on Project Xena. Honestly, you could've done better."
I keep my hands on the keys. "I met the project requirements. It passed all tests."
He studies me for a moment, then smirks. "You could have done better."
Words jam. Heat drains from my arms; shoulders fold. I start to shrink.
Steve pivots in his chair, a flat look between us.
Tom holds the stare a moment longer, before returning to his desk.

"Don't take it personally. He's like that with everyone," Steve says.

My shoulders unhook; heat returns to my arms.

That afternoon, late light bands across Greg's office door. He waves me in; the door clicks shut softly.

After we go over the status of my tasks, I ask,

"Did I meet the requirements for Xena?"

"You did. Field trials are rock-solid—great job, as always."

"Tom said I should've done better."

"That's Tom being Tom." A pause. "You've got good ideas, but your voice is too low in the room. No one really teaches that part in school—how to deal with all kinds of personalities, some of them are difficult. I'll email you a few book recommendations."

With Tom, I fold the way I did at school—same old reflex. But this time, the space around me is different. Greg names my work as solid, encourages me to find my voice, offers books instead of blame. My nervous system begins to rewire—strength surfacing through the same current that once carried fear; weaving itself into confidence. I am learning to stand my ground.

Male authority doesn't crush; it anchors.

—————————————————

A month later, with fresh bills crackling in my pocket, I drive to the bike shop whose page I've starred. The bell rings—rows of glinting bicycles. At once I see her: a crimson Trek 1200.

"May I?"

The clerk nods. Outside, one push, and the frame clicks into alignment. Pedal, rise. Breath fuses to chain. Immediately I understand: this is my first self-chosen love. Five hundred dollars land on the counter; something old shears away, a new shoreline emerges beneath my feet—no longer anchored to my parents' wallet.

Most evenings I roll onto the backroads of Northwest Atlanta. The first slope ignites my quads; pine-scented wind unfurls across my chest; only gear-clicks and cricket choirs thread the silence.

In the long quiet between each pedal stroke, I hear Samira's laughter—cedar-bright, noon-warm—then catch the scent of jasmine in her hair, a fragile plume threading softly through the spokes. Some nights the memory tilts so vividly I reach back, half-expecting her hand to close over mine, steady as it once had been.

———————————

A week later, after work, we drift to the ground-floor lounge bar—low light, backlit bottles, a long bar on one side, and banquettes wrapping the edges. Couches tuck into corners. Small tables glow with tea candles. Ice knocks in short glasses; bass from the playlist hums the room together.

Greg posts up near the bar with Mae from Sales, trading trip stories. Steve's laugh rolls in from a corner booth. Tom stands at a high table, telling his best customer-success stories.

Rina taps the cushion beside me and slides in.

"Off-hours you," she says, smiling. "Slower pace, more relaxed."

"Something like that." I lift my pint of stout.

She settles beside me, her posture open. We keep talking. She shares that she's single, an only child with conservative parents. I tell her I'm the youngest kid, from Lahore, and single. The conversation flows easily, companionable, more friendship than spark.

Steve appears at the edge of the booth with two beers. He sets one by my hand. "Hike Saturday? River loop."

"Yes," I say right away. "Early."

"Perfect." He taps the can to mine and moves on.

Rina watches him go, then looks at me. "Bring me along sometime. I'm slow uphill and talk too much on the flats."

"Deal." The word lands easy.

Around us, the room breathes—clink, loud talk, a saxophone line threading the mix.

Pines breathe resin, the river hushes below, winding through the same red-clay switchbacks I once walked with Ismail. Beside me, Steve keeps an easy pace. He's handsome, athletic, five years older than me. Work and hobbies flow easily between us; I tell him about my new bicycle, and he gets excited about riding together. My body stays with me—heels weighted, calves warm; I feel no pull to borrow his maleness. His openness carries no charge beyond friendship—no signal of invitation, neither emotional nor physical. We move along the trail, distinct, untroubled; the only hunger in me is for the hills.

Morning arrives gentle, my body rested. Another Monday, another gym day. As always, inside the locker room I walk narrow and small, eyes fixed on the floor. Shoulders tense at the risk of a naked flank grazing the edge of vision. I keep moving—small steps, careful breath—holding myself tight. Inside, I feel like a boy in a room full of men who never had to master the art of disappearing.

I had never been around naked men. Where I grew up, men didn't undress beyond their underwear in front of each other. When Asif touched me, it was always at night, in the dark, under a blanket. In the U.S., locker rooms hit me with a strong, confusing charge; I am afraid of what it means.

Next weekend I walk into a porn shop—first time.
Hands shaking. Breath high and thin. I grab straight, bi, gay—anything to name the charge. At the register, bills flutter. The cashier's look is puzzled. He has no idea what's happening inside. Neither do I.

A year unfurls: code, bonuses, recognition, new friends, dusk-lit rides. Projects across teams; Rina joins a few, and our friendship grows. Work does more than keep time—it roots me in fresh American ground. Business-class flights and sunlit boardrooms give me air I haven't breathed before, while steady praise prunes the thorny undergrowth of my Lahore past.

The phone is cold in my hand, edges biting my palm. I key the numbers; each beep lands too loud. A chill runs up my arm as I pace. The line rings—once, twice, three, four. My thumb hovers over End.

A click. Air. Then her voice—Samira's.
"Faraz here."
Silence.
"How are you, Samira?"
"Well."
"I'm so sorry for what you went through," I say, eyes wet.
"You shouldn't have called me; it isn't appropriate. I'm married."
"I want to meet you, please. I think about you all the time."
"It was only a childish crush. I wish you well, Faraz."
Her voice softens but stays steady.

"I've made peace, and I have a daughter to care for. Please don't call me again."

The line goes quiet. The screen dims. The phone sits heavy in my hand.

I set the phone down and step onto the balcony. The rail is cool; below, the river drags a slow braid of light through the dark. Something in me shears—I choke, then bawl, hands to my face, shoulders shaking. The night answers with a far-off siren and the hush of water on stone. The river goes on—no verdict, no lesson—just motion, endless and indifferent, until I watch long enough for the ache to thin and breath to return.

Chapter 11

Ages 25 to 27

The bedroom is dim—streetlight on the curtains, a fan ticking slow. I slide under the sheet to sleep. Missing finds me fast. Samira's face rises; tears follow. I let them come, quiet, the pillow taking salt.

My mind goes to her—how she'd tip her chin when she laughed, the warmth that steadied my chest. My hand drifts to my groin, my body answers halfway, then stalls. The wanting is there—I can't get fully hard. I think about giving up—then don't.

I sit up, reach into the closet, and pull out the VHS tapes I bought at the porn shop. The TV washes the room blue; the VCR whirs; a tape slides in with a clack. Snow, then picture.

A man and a woman. Heat returns. My body stirs. Blood rises—but my eyes pull toward the man, not the woman. The camera lingers on her. Not him.
I want raw male bodies. Wild. Out of control. Explicit.
I swap tapes. Two men. On the screen.
My first time watching two men together.

The charge hits. Sudden. Bright. Confusing.
Energy moves through me—a current I can't map.
I don't know what it means.
I can't stop watching.
My eyes lock on their bodies. In action.
Body parts. Zoomed in. Focused.
I'm fully aroused.

My body learns to remember maleness from pixels—low risk,
on my terms.
I stroke—trying to imagine doing what they're doing.
Images won't hold.

Samira flashes in—the scent of her body rising like jasmine in
warm air, the texture of her skin alive beneath my palm, her
weight settling against me, her lips softening into mine.

I reach for the remote and click the TV off. I stay hard, eyes
closed.

Just Samira and I. Mouth to mouth. Breath to breath. Release
comes in the full-body memory of her—scent, skin, breath,
embrace.

I lie there, chest rising, and listen to my pulse cool.

Next weekend I'm in the library's sexuality aisle. A worn
paperback graphs the Kinsey scale: 0 to 6, neat boxes, tidy
arrows. I run a finger down the chart and try myself on like
a size—maybe bi? It doesn't sit. The book insists orientation
equals which gender turns you on. Nothing about arousal
wired by trauma.
My head says "bisexual"; my body's a compass

needle—spinning—no north. Still, I photocopy the Kinsey page, slip it into my notebook, and leave with cold hands.

Steve and I fall into a steady rhythm of rides: weeknight river loops, longer climbs on Saturdays. Beside him my body continues to feel whole and unthreatened—nothing to borrow. His strength doesn't eclipse me; it wakes my own: steadier breath, legs asking for hills, a hunger for sleep and food that restores me. With Steve, my nervous system learns a new association: male company as regulation and repair, not craving.

One Friday evening, the afterglow of a fifty-mile ride with Steve still warms my body, pine air sharp in my lungs, I play a voicemail from Rina: *Found a trail by the river. Flat, shady, short. Saturday?*
I reply, "Yes."

Saturday morning the trail is cool and green—flat, shaded, damp leaves sweetening the air. Gravel ticks under our shoes. Dragonflies stitch the light.

Rina lifts a hand from the trailhead map. "Short loop," she says, grin quick, eyes bright. My legs still hum from yesterday's fifty miles with Steve; lungs feel clean. We fall into an easy pace.

Gravel ticks underfoot as we trade light talk—steep grades, favorite loops. Weekend plans, half-finished books, the new downtown café—topics that float and fade between breaths. Our pace evens; the chatter hums with the river.

An easy silence holds—trust implicit.

She nudges a pebble off the path. "Being an immigrant's child…it's heavy," she says, half-smiling. "My parents carry this picture around—Gujarati husband, two kids, a cul-de-sac. Sometimes I wonder if I exist to them outside that frame."

We step over a root. She adds, lighter, "I've been lucky, though. Aunties, uncles, cousins—the whole Atlanta web. Potlucks every other Sunday. Somebody always dropping mangoes at the door. That net kept me afloat when I was the only brown girl in class."

"What was that like?" I ask.

She tightens her ponytail, thinking. "Nothing dramatic. Just…constant. Kids holding their noses at my lunch. Teachers chewing my last name into a different shape. Little jokes that weren't little." She glances at me, then back to the trail. "I'd come home furious. My parents love me, but they didn't have the words. 'Ignore it. Study harder.' That was the playbook."

She goes on, softer: "At school I learned to shrink; at home I learned to sparkle. The whiplash wore me out." She taps the arm of her glasses. "And now, in meetings, there's this quiet voice that checks me: 'Be agreeable. Don't be too much.' Which is funny, being in marketing."

"For what it's worth," I say, "I hear you clearly in the room."

"I know." She gives me a quick, grateful look. "That's why I can say this to you."

"Enough about me, what about you? How was life in Pakistan?" she asks.
I give her the outline, not the complete story: a hard childhood, a lost love, a breakup I still carry.

"Thank you for trusting me," she says, voice low, hand warm on my arm.

The trail bends toward sunlight, and with it, the moment quietly exhales to an end.

Next week Tom swings by my desk.
"Did you make the improvements I suggested?"
"My code meets the requirements. Unless priorities change, I'm moving to the next task."
Hands still. Shoulders loose. Eye contact, one beat; back to work.
"Fair enough. Just keep stretching yourself—you'll thank me later."
He drifts on. The cursor blinks. I keep my pace.

As weeks become months, Rina and I keep choosing each other—chemistry quiet, warmth gathering—respect and unspoken trust holding. Saturdays we work the Midtown food bank—pallets of rice, flats of canned tomatoes—Rina earnest without show, learning names, meeting each person's eyes, her care landing as respect, not charity. On walks home, she tells me why she likes being around me—real, not performative; sharp at work without needing to win the room. We both like keeping the parts of our culture that feel like home. Our goodbyes start to linger: a longer hug, her hand at my forearm, my palm at her back, the easy fit of washing dishes shoulder to shoulder. On the couch we sit close, knees touching; her head finds my shoulder. The more we volunteer and hike, the more I share—all of my childhood trauma, the sexual abuse, the story of Samira, and the break it left behind. She listens without flinching.

I don't tell her about my attraction to men. I open my mouth once, twice, but the words dissolve before they reach air. My chest clamps, throat dry. It isn't hiding—it is that my body cannot form language.

One evening after we finish our chai, she guides me into her bedroom, dimly lit by the glow from outside. A raw current surges through my muscles, craving open throttle, but her single word—"Gentle"—pulls the reins tight. Desire shrinks to a controlled burn: strength funneled into careful, one-way strokes; passion kept polite. She lies mostly still, eyes soft, receiving, while my pulse hammers against the bit of its own restraint. When we still, her cheek rests over my heart, and the creature inside me curls around its unspent roar.

I want our sex wilder—raw, unguarded, like with Samira, maybe more. And yet I love Rina; her kindness and authenticity hold my heart. Even so, underneath, a harder truth runs: I stop reaching for women whose chemistry matches mine because my confidence in my manhood has thinned. The pull toward Ismail and the arousal to gay porn leave me feeling less solid—unsure I can carry a relationship that burns hotter.

I'm about to turn twenty-seven. I decide to propose to Rina. For years my trust has been mishandled—by family, by friends, by the way things ended with Samira. With Rina, the ground holds: three Atlanta years of work, river trails, food-bank shifts, and her steady presence when I've spoken the hardest parts. Our chemistry burns lower than the fireworks I want. But this flame is clean, durable. It lights rooms, not brushfires. I want to stand before her and choose a life I didn't inherit—a marriage built on trust and shared values.

I decide to tell my family in person. After five years, I fly back.

Lahore—afternoon heat, fan ticking. Mother pours tea; Father watches; Ashi leans in.
"I'm getting married," I say. "Her name is Rina."

Mother's hand stills over the sugar bowl. "Is she Muslim?"
"No," I say. "Her family is Hindu."

Father's mouth tightens. "You'd marry a non-Muslim? Shameful."
Ashi adds softly, "What a social disgrace."

I keep my breath even. "I am marrying her. I'll send the invitations."

Silence. Cups touch saucers.

That night I end the visit early and fly home.

On the coast of Savannah, wind lifts the vows. A crowd from work fills the rows; Rina's parents sit near the front, while twenty of her aunties, uncles, and cousins arrive with hugs and mango jokes. Huma and Nimra come too, side by side, formal, polite, keeping to the edge. The ceremony is a braid—marigold garlands and a touch of rosewater, rings and English vows, samosas beside a tiered wedding cake—Gujarati, Pakistani, American. We say yes with salt air on our faces.

Chapter 12

Ages 27 to 30

The backyard sits warm and green—grill smoke in the air, laughter moving across the grass. Rina's parents, aunts, uncles, cousins, drift in simple loops: aunts loading the table—ten of them, uncles comparing grocery prices. An Urdu ghazal mixes with a reggae beat.

Rina's mom presses tongs into my hand. "Turn the skewers." An uncle hands me a spoon of sauce, waiting for my read. Her dad lines up beside me at the grill. On the lawn, two little cousins set up a backyard game and ask me to pitch. I toss an easy one; they rocket it into the bushes. We cheer. Across the yard Rina lifts her chin: You good? I raise the tongs.

It reminds me of my childhood in Sialkot—same calm, same sun—only this time without the stress. Just day, food, people glad to be together.

Rina scans the yard, smiling. "These are the moments I live for," she says. "Everyone together—and you with us. One of the best days of my life." She steps in, hugs me, a light kiss. When she pulls back, her eyes stay on mine to make sure I get it.

The house is quiet again. Plates stacked, counters damp, the soft hush of the dishwasher starting up.

"I wish Nimra and Huma were here too," Rina says.
My mouth tightens. "You know how hard it is for me around them," I say. "I'd be braced the whole time. I couldn't enjoy today. Your family isn't mine—but they love me, and I love them. I've never felt this kind of belonging before."

She steps in, arms around me, a quick kiss. I want to lean into it, but my chest won't unclench.
"I know," she says. "Maybe it's time to forgive a little. Make peace. We could visit Huma and Nimra."
"I had a great time," I say, forcing the words quieter than I mean to. "Let's not pull me back there tonight."
She holds my eyes. "Family matters to me. I want yours in our life the way mine is in yours."
I set the towel down, fingers tight on the damp cotton. The dishwasher hums, loud in the silence, a sound I can't tune out.

Three years into our marriage. Most Sundays, Rina's parents swing by. He levels a shelf, oils a hinge; she fills the fridge—"for our week." Fridays stretch late with her cousins: bodies loose on the couch, stories traded until midnight, the house quiet and warm. Weekends brim with people—cousins, friends, her parents again—group hikes, potlucks, long drives to the coast with the windows down and salt in the air.
Their love lands as calm. It's what I lacked as a child. Here, I have it—often, openly. And I am happy. And I am thankful.

At night I stay within her gentleness. She lies open and soft; I keep my strength trimmed to fit. When I ask for more—more edge, more give-and-take—she strokes my face and whispers, "Stay with me, like this, please don't change this." Love gathers at my throat. So does guilt. Wanting more feels like betrayal, so I press the wanting down. The room stays tender, almost perfect. My body stays half-muted.

Some nights a surge rises with nowhere to land. If thoughts of men flare and Rina is beside me, I redirect—fix on her breath, her weight, and let desire settle there. If I'm alone, I spark arousal with a male image, then pivot to a woman and finish. I don't watch porn.

What I can't register yet: part of my sexuality still lives in dissociation. Safe intimacy with women routes that energy along its native path. Back then I didn't know why a wilder charge kept calling. I didn't know that stronger, mutual chemistry hauls more of my traumatized sexuality back into my body—if only briefly—and lets me reclaim some power that abuse stole.

By day I'm rooted; by night I'm careful. I call it maturity—partly true.

One night, dinner plates sit drying on the rack. Rina wipes the counter, then turns, towel in hand.

"I've been thinking about a baby," she says. "I want one."
"I do too." I glance at the window—night reflected back at me. "Honestly, I'm not ready."
She leans against the counter. "Say more."
"The trauma still runs in the background," I say. "It feels like something was taken from me and I can't get it back. I feel less of a man. I don't want to hand that to a child."

She sets the towel down, steps closer. Her voice softens. "I love you. You're not inadequate. My family loves you; your team at work respects you." A pause. "You've carried so much alone. I'm proud of you. Maybe it's time for help—therapy?"

After a long pause: "Thinking about it makes me anxious—it brings everything back. Let me sit with it."

The routines hold: groceries, lists, movie nights. Beneath them, the anxiety hums.

Then I dream:

I balance on a razor ledge above a sea of rot. Just as I tip toward the black water, a warm wind rises and carries me to a shoreline of golden sand.

A robed man waits there, dusk in his eyes.

I am naked yet unafraid, rest my head in his lap like a child; his love pours into me, warm as liquid sunlight, streams through my veins.

I wake before dawn glowing, every cell thrumming. I don't know why—only that something in me shifted. The decision lands clean: therapy. By lunch, the first intake is on the calendar.

Chapter 13

Ages 30 to 33

The waiting room hums with white noise and carpet cleaner. Vida appears—tall, early forties, gaze neither hunting nor retreating. Her office holds two chairs, no desk, and a lamp casting a soft glow.

Over sessions, Vida takes history—birthplace, school, Samira, work. At "childhood," my throat locks; tears erase words. She doesn't push. "Feet on the floor. Name what you see." Lamp. Window. Chair. I restart, stall again—long blanks. We set the order and pace: body first, story second, slow.

Before I leave, she asks, "Draw one childhood scene that still lives in your body."

That night I sketch my first day of school: two older boys peel me from the crowd—elbows, lunch tins, heat—and a fist folds my gut. On the porch, the boy—me—retches, mute. During the next session, the drawing comes to life—tears come fast, then fear, then a hollow ache I can't name.

Therapy becomes a weekly orchestration of my childhood—pages rearranged, grief unbound. Vida holds the room steady—kind, calm, almost expressionless; no matter what I say, her face carries quiet compassion.

After several weeks, I say his name: Asif.

The air hardens. I give her the outline—age, rooms, pattern, the silence after. When I look up, Vida is unchanged: calm, compassionate. As if what I just said were no different from everything before.

Looking back, I realize I wanted a reaction that matched what I shared—something that could make room for the fear and shame inside me. I craved attunement—her meeting my feelings so what I carried could feel held and start to move.

When I tell her I'm attracted to men, Vida says it's a common aftereffect of sexual trauma—"It doesn't make you gay." Her words confirm what I already knew; the mismatch stays—dread in my chest, body dim, the Ismail obsession that once hijacked my days. She doesn't ask what it feels like in me—no questions about the charge, the numbness, the fear. Her calm stays level. If she's this calm, the blame is mine; what's inside me is the problem—I'm defective.

I ask Vida if Rina can join a session so I can tell her about my attraction to men—the one thing I can't say alone. Vida says yes.

Rina sits beside me, hand warm on mine. Vida sets the frame: "We're naming hard things. We'll keep it slow."

I look at Rina. "I'm attracted to men sometimes." My voice holds. "It's old trauma in my body. I don't think I'm gay."

Vida nods. "This is common for straight survivors. Trauma can wire arousal to male closeness. Arousal doesn't determine identity."

Rina doesn't flinch. "I'm sorry you had to carry that confusion, Faraz. I never questioned your orientation." Her thumb presses my knuckle. "How can I help?"

"It gets confusing," I say. "I've gotten hard watching gay porn. I don't watch porn now, but the pull shows up.
I want more give-and-take in sex. More heat. A little wild. Not to scare you—just to stand in strength trauma took."

"I want you happy," she says. "For me, I like to feel everything as it happens. Slow turns the lights on. 'Wild and crazy' makes me shut down."

Vida steps in. "Different nervous systems, different tempos. Neither wrong. Your job is to find the overlap and build range—one notch at a time, not a switch." She looks at both of us. "Name what each of you wants in plain language. Agree on guardrails. Use a stop word. Try short experiments and debrief."

Rina nods. "I can try more heat if we go in steps."

Vida writes three lines on a card and sets it between us:

1-   Go slow and breathe together; if either of us tenses, we pause.

2-   Faraz ask before turning up the intensity; Rina can say yes, no, or slower.

3-   Our safe word is STOP; when either of us says it, we check in.

We read it together. Rina slips the card into her bag. Her hand finds mine again and stays.

That night I press Huma's number, Houston ringing across a thousand miles.
"Salam," I say.
She replies, "Salam, Faraz. May Allah protect you."
Words hover like sparks. I release them: "Someone molested me when I was a child."
Without missing a beat, she asks,
"Asif?"
The name slices the air like glass. I fold inward, tears flooding the hollow she's just exposed. A stunned thought flares—she didn't ask who, or when. Did she know all along?

She calls the next day. She and her husband spoke to Asif—he admitted it. Her husband wants us to stay quiet. "Think of my household," she pleads, saying he'll make life miserable if word spreads.

When I tell my parents, Nimra, and Ashi, they also believe me. Then comes the counsel: forgive, keep quiet. They trade stories of other kids who've suffered—it's common and life moves on. It lands like a second harm: truth acknowledged only to be buried, my pain muted for their comfort.

"The past can't be undone," they say. "What matters now is keeping Huma happy."

No outrage. No plan. Just a hush made into virtue.

No one asks how the wound has shaped my life.

I cry in Rina's arms like a baby after the call.

I cancel the Pakistan trip we've planned so Rina can meet my parents.

Rina and I follow Vida's card. We slow down, check in, practice edges. There's real progress; there are hard limits. About eighteen months in, Rina raises children again. She's in her early-thirties; waiting longer scares her. She also sees how deep my trauma goes. I promise I'm giving everything to therapy. I am.

My body says otherwise. Daylight fills with dread that has no object. On the road I keep twisting to the rearview, certain a car is shadowing me. At green lights I hesitate. In parking lots I scan rows twice, keys tight between my fingers. Grocery store—aisles feel like traps.

Vida's tools don't land.

I white-knuckle work—deliver on time, smile on cue. At home I unravel: tears on the kitchen floor, sobs that shake the frame.

Rina rubs my back, brings water, sits through the storms until she can't. Her kindness frays into exhaustion; I fold into guilt.

Behind the chaos, it's simple: I need to go. Not because love failed, but because staying crushes the space I need to heal. I couldn't explain it—only feel it.

A year later, we start couples therapy. Over months, we see our wants divide. I need space for healing; she wants a child—now. In bed, our tempos drift apart.

One evening, the lamps low, Rina says, "I still believe in what we built, Faraz. You taught me how to be seen without performing. But I can feel you drifting toward a world I can't follow—not because I don't love you, but because it's your own healing now."
Her voice trembles. I take her hand. "You were the first place I ever felt safe."
Tears blur her eyes. "Then let that be what we keep," she whispers. "Let's not wound it by holding on too long."
We cry quietly, her forehead against mine, both of us wishing love were enough to stay.
"I wish we could fix this," I say.
"Maybe this is the fixing," she answers.
We stay there a long time, fingers linked, until the silence itself feels like mercy.

We part in love. We text on holidays, send photos of trails. The chapter closes like a door eased shut—no slam, just the click that says we're honest now.

Into the Groove

2000

Chapter 14

Ages 33 to 35

Sunlight pours through the west-facing window, filling the room with soft gold. Dust drifts and dances in the air while Rafi and Bil, my two rescue puppies, burst across the rug. Rafi's rust-and-cream coat catches the light as he bounds toward Bil, whose slate fur shimmers with motion.

The tug-rope stretches between them, pulling taut, twisting, loosening again. A tumble, a leap, a quick dart of laughter in their eyes. When the play slows, they fold to the ground, pressed side by side. Their tongues slip out, their breath deepens. Rafi rests his head on Bil's shoulder; Bil sighs, half-dreaming.

I kneel beside them. The air is warm and whole. No task waits, no weight presses down—only this bright pause where the world feels simple and kind.

Watching them, my body remembers freedom and safety; some exiled pieces of my childhood return home.

Dinner dishes rinse clean, cumin-and-rice steam drifting. I stand at the sink, palms warm, forearms loose, heart unknotted.

The house holds a cradle-like quiet—the kind that contains, never confines.

Back in the living room, Rafi waits, tail low and sure; Bil stretches long. We pad toward the bedroom, paws and feet muffled on wood. Under lamplight I curl onto my side, breath sinking into my ribs. Rafi tucks against my belly, grounding weight; Bil presses along my spine, sealing warmth.

Their heat seeps into me, loosening the small knots that guard my chest. The air slows around us. A quiet pulse moves through fur and skin—steady, familiar, wordless. My body answers without thought: heart easing, muscles giving in. They soften too, breathing into my warmth. A sweet innocence fills the hush of night.

Our breaths braid—three slow currents—and lull us to sleep.

After ending things with Rina, I craved new ground. I trade sticky Georgia heat for Silicon Valley's surge, moving to the headquarters of the company I work with. The Valley thrums like a spring flood—and I step into the torrent grinning, eager to feel the new current under my bare soles. I rent a small single-family house in Mountain View, its rooms echoing at first, waiting to be filled with breath, paw steps, and life.

———————————

Three months in, Sohail—my new boss, a Pakistani immigrant—calls me into his office.

"I hear you're a rock star," he says. "I've seen your decks—clean, sharp. We need help on customer-facing work. Greg and your old team say you're a fit."

"I've sat in on those meetings," I tell him. "Questions get tough—sometimes aggressive. I get nervous."

"Fair," he says. "Let's train the nerves. Two-week workshop on presenting under pressure. It helps."

The offer lands clean; my shoulders drop. "Yes," I say. "I want that."

Another supportive boss—one step closer to reclaiming my power. I step into the hall with a grin.

The workshop is small—eight of us with two top-notch psychologists, corporate communications specialists. They record us as we present, then play the tapes back, guiding us through body language and tone. I learn that even when I feel like I'm collapsing inside, it doesn't show nearly as much as I fear. I also learn I'm far from alone—everyone battles their own version of stage fright, and some have it even stronger than I do.

———————————

I feel the pull long before my eyes register the storefront. East-West Bookstore sits only a few blocks from home, yet crossing its threshold feels like entering a different world—a universe of honeyed incense and buzzing pages. Spines tower overhead—shelves of breathwork, craniosacral therapy, and trauma healing—worlds I haven't named but have been scent-tracking for years. I drift aisle to aisle on instinct alone.

A crimson flyer on the community board catches my eye—*Brotherhood Weekend*. It promises a reset of your manhood, a lift to every relationship—starting with yourself—and a call to show up as partner, father, and brother you were born to be.

Male intimacy always ripped me open—longing clawed at my gut, dread ground against bone, arousal crackled through raw nerves—while the rest of me vanished, sucked into a private black hole. But the word *brotherhood* strikes like rain on parched roots, hinting at fertile soil deep enough to anchor and nourish me.

With no obligations to dam the current, I register.

Late-afternoon light pools across the clearing. Pine-scented dust softens underfoot as forty of us stand shoulder to shoulder, forming a broad circle. We begin the first exercise: hands resting on the next man's neck and back, each breath syncing until the ring feels like one slow-beating lung.

I learn that I'm not alone in my trauma—far from it. Raw confessions spill into the open air; whenever grief surfaces, arms close around the speaker to anchor. One man's tremor draws another's steady palm. Weight shifts, tears fall, and the earth drinks them, turning grit to loam beneath our feet.

Men holding one another like this—without mockery, without retreat—rewires my nervous system. Safety, acceptance, tenderness: a current I never imagined could pass between us.

A facilitator calls for the "trust fall," only the catch involves twenty hands instead of two. I step to the center, heart hammering, stone-hard, and let myself tip backward. Twenty arms catch me in a soft, interwoven crash—heat, sweat, muscle, heartbeat—the first time male contact feels trustworthy. When they ease me upright, I stay inside my body, solid and spacious, surprised to find my breath unbroken.

By the time the weekend ends, I already crave the current that carries me—addicted to the clean rush of safe male contact.

I find a men's circle in Mountain View that meets every Wednesday evening, and soon we sit on chairs arranged in a circle. We open with steady breath, then take turns sharing our stories. Each man listens fully; each response meets the speaker with care and respect: *What do you need?* Arms wrap around shoulders, palms rest on backs, grief and laughter pass hand to hand. The touch is simple—grounded, permissioned—and every time it lands, my body drops a little deeper into itself, anchoring in the places it once fled.

Within two months I've told them everything. I say, "Will you support me when I call Asif? When I picture it, my heart rockets, my mind whites out, and I feel like I could drop." José, Caleb, and Mark answer without hesitation: "Yes—honored." They offer to come to my place and sit with me while I make the call.

A few days later, I make the call.
As I tap the numbers, my throat goes dry. My coccyx and the base of my neck throb as if they might crack; fear tears through my gut. I slide onto the carpet and ask Mark to sit back-to-back with me—I need a safe body against mine. José and Caleb press in at my sides, a steady hold. My body loosens; breath returns. Rafi and Bil nose in and curl against my legs.

I hit speaker. Ring. Click.
"This is Faraz."
A beat. Then his voice: "How are you, son? I hope all is well."

Son. My mouth locks. José squeezes my shoulder; I'm not alone.
"Why did you hurt me?" I ask.
"I'm sorry," he says. "I shouldn't have. But you must remember—you were equally responsible."

The words land and, for a second, feel true. I start to fold. I end the call.

I break. Mark, Caleb, and José pull me in and hold until the shaking passes. Rafi and Bil lick the salt from my face. The room stays with me until my breath evens.

In the days after, I speak with two Pakistani lawyers about suing Asif. Both are blunt: the laws are weak; enforcement is rare. The call ends with my jaw tight and hands cold. Justice won't come from a court; the work drops back to my body, my circle, my breath.

———————————————

Caleb mentions a Vipassana meditation retreat two hours north—curiosity ripples through my chest. Two weeks later I'm in a white-walled hall where silence is the only language. Ten silent days plant a seed, and it keeps sprouting after the retreat.

At home, I practice—thirty minutes at dawn, twenty at lunch. When Caleb invites me to the Monday-night Vipassana group, I slip into the circle; week after week, the gathering becomes another anchor of my new life.

Vipassana trains attention on bodily sensations. We experience everything through the body. Every experience first arises as sensation in the nervous system's oldest circuitry—the reptilian brain. Then it moves into the limbic system and becomes feeling—fear, anger, grief, warmth—and finally shapes thought and behavior. I call this the **body → feeling → story** arc: sensation first, then feeling, then story.

Understanding the **body → feeling → story** sequence became the foundation of my healing—the nervous system's three-part engine for experiencing life.

Trauma carves grooves into that chain. To survive, I learned to feel only what was pleasurable; everything else was bypassed. Trauma also breaks the chain, leaving unbearable experiences trapped—either unfelt or circling in the same pocket of discomfort, instead of flowing through and integrating with the rest of the body. A healthy body is like a river—continuous, interconnected, alive.

The work is to notice sensations and stay with them—steady, attentive, not pulled away by thought or impulse. Stay long enough, and the nervous system begins to learn a new **body → feeling → story** path—less past, more present.

Somatic psychology and old contemplative teachings both point to the same truth: when awareness meets sensation without agenda, the system reorganizes itself. The body remembers its native rhythm. Some call this kind of seeing *non-interfering awareness.*

Trauma disrupted my natural flow of arousal, carving **body** → **feeling** → **story** paths for survival. Without support, the ruts deepened—sex braided with dissociation. Insight didn't change it. Healing meant rejoining arousal to embodiment, choice, and safety.

————————————

Father calls. His voice is careful: Mother has liver cirrhosis. The doctors say a year, maybe two. Grief and tenderness braid in my chest. Whatever the history, I love her. The child in me reaches for his mother.

————————————

Practice needs play. One Friday, belly full of pho on Castro Street, I drift into dusk as a thump-thump-thump—earthy drums—rises from the sidewalk. My stride syncs: step-step-jog. The beat thickens with wild sax; sparks of sound skitter through the night. I follow it to an old church hall flinging music out its windows like holy confetti. A sign on the door makes it plain: *Dance of Liberation—free-form dance every Friday.*

Inside, dim lights glaze the varnished floor while a hundred bodies spin and whoop in ruleless motion, a collective heartbeat shaking the rafters. Shoes off, soles warm, I hover for a breath, then the crowd's tide pulls me in. Hips ignite, shoulders roll, spine ripples, breath locks into the downbeat, primal cries erupting. Faces blur—laughing, eyes closed—and movement no longer belongs to anyone.

Free-form ecstatic dance gives me a body-centered way to heal. In a room without choreography or talk, I let sensation move me. What I couldn't express as a child—anger, grief, joy—moves now as dance, stillness, and primal sound. Clear consent and simple boundaries build trust; I choose when to be solitary and when to connect.

Paired with Vipassana, the work lays trauma-free tracks along the **body → feeling → story** chain. Vipassana builds awareness; dance gives it motion.

Vipassana is awareness meeting stillness.
Dance is awareness meeting movement.
Both are vehicles of liberation—one thaws trauma, the other stitches it back into tissue. Two wings of the same bird.

I didn't know why I left Rina and a life full of love. Now I do. My body had its own healing plan. When I didn't listen, it spoke in vigilance—rearview mirror checks, keys clenched, aisles that felt like traps.
Now I let the body lead. I trust its instincts more than my mind's logic. With that surrender comes a calm, vivid aliveness I've never felt.
Sex stays in the background. I don't pursue sexual contact with men or women; the fantasies are rare now. What feeds me is nonsexual closeness with my brothers and the play of free-form dance—both thawing the frozen child and stitching him back

into muscle and nerve. Work keeps backing me—steady pay, supportive bosses, chances to stand in my strength.

Life aligns to repair what childhood broke. Rafi and Bil remind me daily how to be a wild, carefree kid—always finding reasons to play, connect, be glad. Yoga slips in between—sun salutes at lunch, long lunges after meetings.

For the first time, the truth rises—simple and bright: my body is home.

Chapter 15

Ages 35 to 36

I lay my mat under the skylight as a tall, athletic stranger slips in. He flicks his mat open beside mine; the soft thud lands in my chest. Our eyes meet—brief, startling—and the air tightens.

The practice begins. Breath draws him in; sets him under my skin. I watch the line of muscle in his thighs, the body contained, sure. I hold the pose, trembling. Each inhale draws his heat toward me, each exhale pushes it deeper under my skin. We fold and touch our toes. I glance sideways; desire pools. In the warrior pose, our fingertips almost brush, electricity crackling between us. By the final rest—flat on my back, my pulse is pounding so fiercely that stillness feels like a dam ready to break.

Years of watching, wanting, retreating. Now the body asks to know, not think. To feel what's real.

I brave a coming-out support group for gay men in a church basement off Market Street in San Francisco. Halfway there, my knees jackhammer; the sidewalk tilts like a slipping fault. Breath splinters, sweat pools, nausea rises. At the door I stall—skin buzzing, mind blank—then I take three ragged yogic breaths, steadying the quake enough to descend the narrow stairs.

Inside, voices move through the room—some smooth, others jagged and raw. When the circle turns to me, I say only, "I'm not sure why I'm here—just that I need to be," and the room receives the confession in quiet understanding.

Afterward, I stand in the fog. One of the men from the group approaches—handsome, kind. We find a bar nearby. Over beer, he listens to the bones of my story—never touched a man, terrified. His hand rests on my thigh. He asks, "Want to come to my place?" Deep inside, the body leans toward yes. I cover his hand and speak plainly: "It's very scary for me to be intimate. If we go forward, I want to initiate and decide what I do. You can always say no. And please ask before doing anything different with me."
He nods, steady. My yes feels clean.

Sunlight slants through the wide window, laying a single gold band across the floor. He stands inside it—broad-shouldered, rooted, waiting. I ask if I can undress him and lead; he nods. One by one, I unbutton his shirt, fabric sliding from freckled muscle. I move with reverence, as if seeing a man's body for the first time.

I kneel, loosen his shoes and denim, briefs last—cotton skimming firm thighs—until he steps clear, sun catching the planes of chest and hip. I shed my own clothes, drawn toward him in wordless awe. Slowly we explore—fingertips gliding over collarbone, flank, the taut sweep of thigh—trading in quiet wonder. In his arms, skin to skin, I am whole; nothing to ask, nothing to answer—only the ache for it to last.

He wants to go further. I'm satiated and aroused. I tell him that's as far as I want to go.

Decades of imagining. Then—arrival. Gratitude rises, tidal. I kiss his warm cheeks, then his brow. "Thank you."

Kindness has done its quiet work. Samira's warmth, Rina's love, her family's steady welcome, supportive colleagues—all of it re-teaches my body what safety feels like. They aren't healers, but their care is medicine. It gives me courage to welcome every part of me.

For the first time, I move with ease—unafraid, unguarded. Sexual energy, once padlocked, begins to uncoil; I let myself be with men for a handful of nights, to feel that long-exiled current move. The same pattern repeats—sensual touch and nothing more.

The child I exiled steps into daylight—no judgment, no right or wrong, no healed or unhealed—just free. For weeks I move through Castro—bookshops, espresso. I watch openly, letting others' maleness in—without shame.

One afternoon a sun-warmed Victorian on 19th Street called to me; I signed before doubt could rise.

Six months in, I ride the Muni from the Castro to our downtown office each morning, then braid my evenings from the same currents: a neighborhood men's circle, free-form dance, studio yoga, and a local Vipassana sit. The cadence feels fresh yet familiar.

But the freer my body gets, the more the Vipassana group chafes. I love tracking sensation, but the dogma grates: anger labeled poison, desire branded hindrance. A teacher claims she meditates four hours a day "to stay peaceful"; I wonder what she's masking with that peace—old hurt, anxiety, desire? Their peace begins to ring hollow. My bones crave wild, unruly movement and honest sexual exploration. I leave the Vipassana group.

At home I sit—twenty, thirty minutes at a stretch—and follow sensation through my body, soles to scalp: what stirs here, what moves there. I map presence and absence—the living parts, and the dissociated places, the ones I can't yet feel.

One day after lifting weights at a neighborhood gym, I drift into the sauna: dry heat clasps my skin, joints slacken, breath a low rasp. A man slides onto the cedar bench beside me—runner's legs, trim waist, shoulders that halt my stare. Wordless, we let the air hum—an unseen current beneath the slats. We stretch calves, hips, shoulders—small motions charging the space. Our eyes touch once, brief and careful, as if we've shared a secret; warmth pools low, pulse quickens.

Outside, I offer a handshake.
"Adrian," he says—eyes bright, vowels liquid.
Over coffee we trade the basics: same age, both single. He grew up in San Francisco—liberal parents, always openly gay—no coming-out story to tell.
We decide to date.

He moves with unguarded grace, as if he owns the sidewalk. His fingers find mine; an arm drapes over my shoulders. There's no trauma story behind his ease—and it shows. His smile is clear, unhidden. Nothing in him conceals; he's wholly visible. His openness steadies me.

When he bends to lace his shoes, the hollow at the base of his spine fits perfectly beneath my palms, and he welcomes every touch. In a kiss, his lower lip trembles, then steadies, his taste lingering on my tongue. When we hug, his chest lifts against mine, each breath a quiet proof that what I've longed for is here—warm, alive, impossibly present, my own.

After a week, we tumble onto the bed. We start caressing each other; I disappear into his muscles, the world narrowing to the pulse between us. Thought loosens, borders blur. A pure current carries me beyond myself, merging with him. I sink into his embrace until nothing of me remains—only an immense, sensual pleasure, my body a single trembling nerve tuned to the thrum of his masculine body. For those moments, I am nothing but his heat and rhythm—no separate self, only the throb and weight of his body.

Adrian wants more, but I'm quenched by the warmth of touch and kisses—nothing beyond that.

Over the next days, he folds me into his friends' circle. "They love you," he laughs, "you make the room breathe easier." The words loosen something—an opening in me that finally meets itself.

That year, my body has the resources to navigate physical intimacy with a man; earlier, I would have reenacted trauma—having sex in unsafe situations without realizing it. Therapy, movement, and Vipassana have shifted my baseline.

With Vipassana, a part of me is always observing sensation. It's an automatic background process slowly reorganizing my system. New pathways form alongside the old grooves.

Adrian is easy in his body and clear in his orientation—no sideways pull, no hidden agenda—and around him I can fully relax. Because I couldn't feel my full experience with Asif, my body seeks safe situations where the same pathways the abuse carved can light up again—only this time on my terms: choice, safety, control. And I never want more physical intimacy than I had with Asif. It's the only kind my body knows.

Being intimate with muscular men is euphoric. My nervous system drinks in their current through the warmth of our embrace. For those minutes it feels mine; I am whole. It reads as sexual identity clarity. I don't know any of this then. I only know I feel the freest I've ever felt—men who want me as I am, rooms that welcome me.

I say, *I'm gay*—and the relief arrives as belonging.

Chapter 16

Ages 36 to 37

I key the old sequence by heart—country, city, home. Ring, ring. A ceiling fan I can't see turns in my head.

"Hello?"
"Salam, Dad. It's me."
"Salam, son."
"I'm visiting," I say. "I want to see Mother."
A small click of teeth on the receiver. "We'll be glad to see you. She misses you—talks about you all the time."
"There's one more thing," I say. "Something new since I left Rina."
"I am listening."
"I've always felt confused about my sexuality. I've been exploring." I breathe. "I am gay."

Silence widens—room to room. Then words tumble—"no... nonsense... shame..."—metal cups clattering across tile. Finally: "You are dead for us."

My hand goes cold on the phone.
"I still want to visit. Mother doesn't have much time."

"You can," he says. "But I can't guarantee your safety. You know what people do to men like you."

The threat enters through my bones. A blow I wouldn't see.

"Tell Mother I love her," I say.
"We will pray for you."

The line dies. I stand with the phone to my ear until the dial tone floods the room.

The kettle finishes its hiss. I pour tea exactly the way she did and watch steam lift, then fade. My ticket search sits open. My body votes. It's not safe.

Next day, Mother and sisters echoed the same sentiment.

I don't go.

Three months later, Ashi calls before dawn. "She's gone." The word lands, small and total. I sit on the bed edge, hand on the phone, listening to the city wake around the space where her voice should be.

Then one day, back couch at a Castro bar. Low light, clink of glasses. Adrian turns to me.

"We've been affectionate, even sensual, but we stop there. I'm curious why."

I tell him the map, plain: what happened with Asif; then Malik; Samira, Ismail, Rina; even the fantasies.

He nods. "I don't want to box you in, but... do you think of yourself as gay? Or are you still figuring it out?"

"I've told my family and close friends I'm gay," I say with a grin. "Still figuring out what that means."

He holds my gaze. "I really like you, Faraz. I don't want to rush you. If someday you want to explore more—with me—I'll be here."

"Thank you," I say. "That means more than you know."

I love being around Adrian, but away from him, ease shatters. I miss him with knife-edge hunger, each hour split open; desk chatter, leash walks, email pings—every path loops back to his scent, his weight. The wanting isn't tender; it's feral, jittery, unlivable, scattering focus like dry leaves.

Some days I drift so far I overshoot my Muni stop, surfacing in unfamiliar neighborhoods, keys sweating in my palm. Only Adrian steadies me; I've fed on his male current so long it hits like a fix. Inside his radius I click into place; outside it I rattle.

I called it love; it was dependence—I used his body to feel what mine couldn't.

We try to be more intimate—after dinners, after dancing, in the quiet of his room. Skin to skin, I light up; but as soon as we reach past sensual touch, the current slips. I want to go farther—to stake a place in the gay community, to live where all of me feels welcome. My body holds the line; arousal drops. It runs on rules I can't override. Within weeks, Adrian ends it.

I keep trying—bar hookups, yoga classmates, friends of friends. Attraction sparks. Then the moment tips toward more and the current slips. I wait for my body's yes. It never comes.

With women my body knows what to do beyond arousal. With men, arousal is the endpoint. Day by day the contrast sharpens, and I let it—no pushing, no verdict, trusting my body to steer.

I stay in San Francisco one last month—just me, Rafi, and Bil. We log miles: they sniff and pull; I sort through what's left. In that quiet I get clear—I need more healing. When the month ends, I move south to Mountain View, back to the same streets and trails.

Chapter 17

Ages 37 to 39

Friday evening at Valley Fair Mall. I want coffee. The line snakes past the counter. I step to the end, not seeing that it turns the corner.

A shadow falls over me. A big, tall man—furious. His voice is a sudden crack of thunder in the mall's din. "The line starts back there!" he roars, jabbing a thick finger around the corner. I want to explain—*didn't see, sorry*—but the words don't form. A tremor starts in my knees, a violent, humiliating shake that races up my spine to my neck. My throat dries.

The fawn response kicks in—my body trying to keep him calm.
Stay small so he won't get madder.
Speaking feels dangerous—what if he attacks?
My body's shaking; I can't protect myself.
He keeps talking but it's all static.

I turn away.
Walk. Tiles. Escalator.
Perfume. Strollers.
Automatic doors.
Air.

The night hits cold. I get to the car, shut the door, and the quiet slams down. I shake. Breath stutters. Then, the sobs come, wracking my body with a force I don't understand.

I stay in the car until the shaking eases. I scan my body, Vipassana-style: soles, calves, hips, belly, chest, throat, jaw. Images flash in my mind—the bed, Asif's room, the child-me. I feel the stuck sensations I couldn't feel then. Now they travel the new pathways built by practice and the kindness of others. Sensation thaws, runs through these channels, and turns into words I couldn't form back then:

Give Asif what he wants.
Who knows what else he's capable of. He might punish me if I say
no.
Become the boy who enjoys this, so Asif feels good.
He's kind in daylight—he must love me.
I love him too.

I must like this, if I don't, then what? I can't fight.
My parents and sister put me in his bed. They trust him.
They won't protect me.
No one will save me.

Alone. Helpless.

So I must do what I can control.
I smile.
I go still.

I call harm love and try to feel only the parts that are bearable—touch, sexual pleasure.

In the driver's seat I meet that boy. One hand on my chest, one on my hips. We are not in that bed anymore.
We can leave. We already did.
Somewhere under the ribs, a small part of me climbs back into the body and stays.

Later that week, I wonder how my experience with Asif has shaped the way I've been with men in the Castro. Was there a *no* I couldn't feel—one I kept overriding while focusing on touch and sexual pleasure? Having sex not from desire, but from the old belief that I didn't have the right to refuse—that I must enjoy it?

Gratitude rises for my work life—for the support it offers, and for the men who meet me with respect. In meetings and reviews, I practice saying what I need to say, this time with the support of authority figures who listen. My bosses, in their steadiness, become a kind of surrogate fathering—helping me finish what was left unfinished.

I find I speak up more easily, hold eye contact longer, ask harder questions. Sohail notices the difference—his smile easy, eyes bright. "You're leading now, not just executing," he says.

My code reviews turn into quiet mentorship sessions; younger engineers gather, asking about deadlines, scope, office politics. I listen and guide. My voice no longer trembles when challenged.

As awareness grows, I can track how attraction shows up. With women I like, warmth rises—cheeks flush, a small happiness settles me; breath drops, feet ground. With men, attraction sparks too, but I feel depleted. It feels coerced—fear dressed as wanting.

So I decide to date women again—to stay in my body.

Rachael's profile: cyclist, easy grin. "Ride hard, breathe deep."
My body trusts motion. I ping her.

We meet on a road ride, wind at our backs, talk sparse. Later, at
the café, her gaze openly traces my sweat-damp jersey, fingers
settling high on my thigh—claiming terrain she already knows
she wants. My pulse quickens, but something inside me isn't
ready yet. I gently cover her hand with mine, smile, and say
clearly, "I need a little more time."

A couple of rides later she invites me back to her place.
The invitation surprises me, but I follow. We sink onto her
couch—quads humming, jerseys faintly salty. She stands beside
me and begins to work my shoulders, slow and deliberate,
thumbs loosening knots I don't know I carry. The touch is
perfect: safe, soothing, and electric all at once. The air between
us thickens; words dwindle; clothes slip away without effort.

My hands skim her skin, but just beneath that ease, something
locks. My heartbeat jumps, pelvis tightens, breath scatters.
When I try to enter her, the current vanishes, as if someone
throws a switch. I draw back, bewildered.

Embarrassment pours in, hot and heavy. Where do I look?
What do I say? A hard voice inside mutters, *What kind of man
stalls at the gate?* Another wonders if old trauma has hijacked the
moment. Yet beneath both is a quieter, sharper truth: my body
had hesitated earlier, and I'd barreled past the signal to prove I
could perform on command—like a man is supposed to.

Later we dress and walk the block, night air cool on our skin. I offer the bare outline of my history—just enough to explain the stall. She listens, polite. At the door she stops, gaze kind yet distant. "I don't have the energy to be with someone carrying that much hurt," she says—clean, almost merciful.

Had our genders been reversed, I wonder, would the words have come out the same?

I tip my head, then slip into the dark—bike weightless, chain whispering—each of us chasing a rhythm our hearts can bear.

A leaden throb seeps through my pelvis, every cell suddenly stamped defective. Outwardly I keep moving, but inside I limp—like a recalled machine: parts misfit, malfunctioning, unfit for the road.

That night sleep hovers just beyond reach. Bil and Rafi flank me on the bed, their breathing steady as ocean swell, but my mind flickers like a broken projector.

First comes the playground: other children chasing, shoving, laughing, and me on the fringe—clueless how to enter their playful world.

Then the reel snaps to my parents' tightening faces, to Asif splintering my desire from my flesh.

Thirty boys tighten the ring, chanting *khusra*—each syllable a flare of triumph meant to scrub me from existence.

Malik, then Ismail, pull at me with magnetism I never choose, never decipher, yet cannot release.

And Samira—first to return my love, to stitch me whole—is torn away; her absence throbs louder than her living warmth ever did.

Even the brief season I call myself gay flickers past: a door marked *welcome* slamming shut as I reach for it.

Straight, gay, bi—every label that might have anchored me to society slips through my fingers.

I lie there, searching for my place in a world that isn't there.

I get desperate and ask around for what might help. Vida gave me language, not relief. I see more therapists. Chairs, couches, small rooms—sometimes no windows. They call it body-first, but the room says sit and talk. I feel most alive on a dance floor; in an office, I can't find that feeling.

No more couches, no more retelling—insight isn't shifting my body. So, no therapy.

A friend from the dance circle says, "Try Shanti, an energy healer in Santa Cruz—everyone swears by her." I write down her name and call her.

She says energy healing is a doorway to hope, a way to reach the pain words can't touch. Hurt—even from past lives—can lodge in the body and shape how I feel now. With light touch or simple movements around the body, she says she can release that old weight so peace and safety can return. The words sound magical; I'm hopeless enough to believe them.

My first appointment looks harmless: amber light pooling, crystals winking along the sill, statues of Lakshmi, Kuan Yin, and Archangel Michael guarding the corners. Lavender—or rose—floating in the air, and a salt lamp glows beside a massage table dressed in white linen. A sanctuary, I thought.

She greets me with a beatific smile and a silent nod, then motions to the table. I climb up slowly: mid-thirties body,

136

thirteen-year-old pulse—hopeful. When I name childhood sexual abuse, she tips her head and moves on—no questions. No anchoring follow-up.

Mid-session she closes her eyes and declares she is reading the Akashic Records, the cosmic ledger of every lifetime. In her vision I'd once been ruthless, powerful. Her voice stays satin-soft. Her lids flutter. Her arms paint fluid arcs in the air. The story mattered less than the performance—poised, theatrical, unassailable.

Visit after visit, she speaks of lifetimes, karma, debt, atonement. I listen—not because it rings true, but because trauma has stolen my compass, and I'm too hopeless to question anything that promises relief. Her suggestions thicken into verdicts: my wounds were earned, my soul fractured long ago, the abuse inevitably my fault. She wields *spirit* to override consent, calling it intuition.

Real healing doesn't descend like oracle speech or bury pain beneath a cosmic story. It lives in relationships: one heart meeting another without flinch, someone choosing to stand beside you—never above. I don't see she's misusing her power; I call it wisdom and believe her. I keep going—to her, then to other energy healers—clinging to any door that opens, until two years pass.

Later I learn she teaches energy healing—and has been crossing sexual boundaries with her students. My men's-group brothers had warned me about energy healers; I couldn't hear it then. When I bring up my concerns, her voice hardens; she says what comes through in session is divinely guided—absolute truth, not open to discussion.

In that moment, the spell breaks. Beatific smile, fluid arms, cosmic claims—stagecraft to keep me small and make her untouchable. Asif's tactic again: call harm love. A clean, cold anger rises. It doesn't shout; it burns through the fantasy that someone else could save me.

Chapter 18

Ages 39 to 42

A week later, a flyer at East West Books catches the light like mica—"Somatic Trauma Healing: Three-Year Program."

The words hum in my gut before I understand them.
I look them up, call, ask my questions, and sign up.

I learn that childhood pain doesn't just live in memory—it lodges in the body, waiting to be stirred awake by a trigger, like what happened to me at Valley Fair Mall.

Somatic psychology is a cousin to Vipassana and to free-form dance—each asks us to listen to the body. Every experience begins as a bodily sensation, before it becomes an emotion, a thought, or an action. But this practice goes deeper, targeting the specific **body → feeling → story** arc that trauma disrupted. Stay with it, and new **body → feeling → story** paths begin to form—ones that respond to this moment, not what came before.

When I stayed with the sensations in the car after getting triggered at the mall, my nervous system began discharging old survival energy—shaking, sobbing, thawing—completing what my body couldn't finish. In that release, a new

body → feeling → story pathway emerged, giving words to what had happened with Asif.

The instructor on the first day says, "The most important thing trauma survivors need to do is feel their anger. Many don't even know they can be angry. Some think it's because they're peaceful—the truth is, they can't feel the sensations of anger because they had to push them down to survive."

He guides us into an exercise. Before we partner up, he sets the container: "This room is safe. Partners are friends." The words land; my shoulders drop.
"Feel anger in the body—its heat, pressure, and drive—without story or thought. Let it move as energy, carving new channels through your nerves. Anger can protect you, set boundaries, become an ally."

Blue mats, bare feet.
"Set your stance," the instructor calls.
My partner—thick wrists, steady gaze—places his palms on mine. Breath swells in my chest.
He leans.
My weight compounds—knees flex, quads ignite. The rubber mat grips my heels; my spine stacks like pylons.
A rumble coils in my diaphragm—primitive, volcanic. On the exhale, I drive forward, arms straightening, torso dropping, voice breaking into a graveled roar. His body shifts, skids, finally yields.

Each drill grants me permission to fight and to guard. With every shove, the baseline shifts—my muscles relearn they can push and still be safe.

That permission illuminates my drift from Buddhist circles that label anger *unspiritual*. For trauma survivors—especially those conditioned to freeze or fawn—embodied anger becomes a doorway to agency: not a flare of rage, but a steady, forging heat that tempers rather than scorches.

I carry that lesson into free-form dance—each stomp, hip-swing, and shout rehearses protection in motion. Rage alchemizes into rhythm, into breath, into belonging.

The other life-changing practice I learn is improvised movement. I quiet my mind—established Vipassana helps tremendously—and I begin to feel bodily sensations, merging with them as if that's all I am: no thoughts, no emotions. It is possible to reach such states with practice.
Then I let my body move and make sounds.
Each movement is different. I never know what gesture or sound will come next.

I step onto the mat and let sensation become music.

My spine sinks into the mat; breath cools at the nostrils, warms in the throat.
Sensation swirls behind the sternum, relaxes the gut, halos the scalp.
I follow the tide inside me.

The flow thickens, tipping me onto my belly.
Impulse—push.
Palms root, toes tuck; wide-armed push-ups drawn by primal intelligence.
Heat climbs—a growl splits into a yell—then a knife-edge scream.

Pressure drains.
Breath steadies into a trembling sigh.

I stand.
Window—sky—sidewalk dissolve into one borderless field: no labels, no edges.

This work becomes especially powerful when it reaches the trauma-shaped circuits of the nervous system—the places where survival energy once froze. These areas hold the charge of what was never completed: the push, the scream, the run, the reach for help that never came. When movement, sound, and attention reach those buried reflexes, the body can finally finish what it began. Energy once locked becomes available for living. Frayed nerves reach to resplice, patient as moss knitting itself over stone.

What happened in the car at Valley Fair Mall was an early example of this process—long before I knew anything about somatic psychology or trauma release. My body found its own way: shaking, crying, thawing. The practice I later learned only gave language and structure to what the body already knows how to do. For many of us, this is the natural rhythm of repair—innate, not taught.

Given real quiet and safety, the body leans toward repair. Trauma persists because our culture grins through pain, shames grief as drama, and worships speed.

The program sparks a somatic rewiring, and it pulses through my body even now.

During the program, I put dating and sex on hold to let my nervous system rewire.

———————————

Thirty faces, a hum of HVAC, the projector's low whirr. I'm mid-slide when the president of a customer's company cuts in—chair scraping, voice hard.

"Fix what you already sold before you try to sell something new."

Heads swivel. Vibration climbs my shins, breath shoots high, throat goes dry. Panic gathers—heat in ears, hands slick.

I find my feet. Toes spread in my shoes. Breath drops to my legs.
Five silent seconds.

I glance to the back. Sohail meets my eyes and gives a small nod, fist clenched in quiet support.

I look at the president, keeping my voice even.
"We'll be happy to schedule a dedicated meeting to discuss your support concerns and make sure they're addressed."

His face reddens; his fist tightens. "Why can't you build better products? Hire better engineers!"

I meet his eyes again—steady, clear, intent.
"Today, we've gathered thirty people to get their feedback, so let's respect everyone's time and stay with the agenda. If

you'd like, we can reserve a few minutes at the end for a brief discussion."

The president leans back. "Please continue."

My heart steps down from a sprint. Spine stacks. I move to the next slide.

On another visit to East West Bookstore, I spot a tower of CDs titled A Secular Guide to Spiritual Enlightenment. Curiosity wins out—I buy a copy, bring it home, and slip the disc into the stereo; the tray glides shut.

A faint pop, a calm—then a voice, measured and unhurried, as though it has been speaking since before my birth. Nothing theatrical, nothing baritone—just a grain that slips between the ribs. Words dissolve; listening alone remains.

The room blurs. I slide to the floor, spine braced against the wall. Thoughts settle into a single warm sheet. Inner chatter drains; even the gay-straight calculus evaporates. For once, nothing begs to be solved.

Ten CDs spin, one after another. Hours pour away unnoticed. Midnight drifts by; still I do not move. At dawn, a blade of silver light crosses the floorboards—I load the next disc, hungry for that voice to gather me again.

Soon the grain is everywhere: in the car, at the desk, above the stove, looping through headphones as I drift to sleep. I spin the series thirty times a year, each listen carving a deeper groove. Eventually I book cross-country flights just to kneel inside his silence, legs numb on retreat-hall floors where days stretch, thoughtless as tundra.

For years I abide by that voice without question. I don't fully know why I follow him. He stirs a memory I can't quite touch, a wordless familiarity that feels like help.

Then a hairline crack opens. He claims that the reality he perceives—one boundless awareness he says he has dissolved into—is the only reality. He insists this is everyone's innermost truth, everything else mere illusion. Doubt coils in my gut.

Who anoints him custodian of everyone's truth?
Why should he chart my terrain better than my own senses?
Why not encourage us to discover a truth as unique as our fingerprints?

During one of his retreats, the veneer thins. Students weave identical teachings into wildly divergent tapestries—some crown themselves "enlightened", others parse semantics until dawn. Insight and imagination look identical.

He certifies his awakening, and his disciples echo him. There is no metric, no glimpse into how "boundless awareness" engages the world beyond the meditation hall. He keeps his personal life sealed off, so students never see how he meets his own unresolved tangles—how he works with conflict, disappointment, or the mess that clings to him off the cushion.

Does it sharpen his courage, move him to speak when injustice roars? In his telling, his liberation floats above worldly chaos, untouched by the demands of the hour. And so the question lingers: what good is boundless awareness if it never leaves the cushion?

I need something earthbound to measure progress.

So I pivot inward. My yardstick becomes congruence: instincts, feelings, thoughts, behaviors clicking into alignment like a quartet finding perfect harmony—each note distinct, the music seamless. I know the pain of inner fracture—when desire pulls one way and the rest of me another.

I stop seeking answers there. The river now surges under its own current, and I trust that pull more than any borrowed current.

My improvised somatic practice outgrows the men's-circle protocol—hands on heart, voice on center—while my body aches to sprawl, quake, rise. Folding chairs hem me in; grief wants to lie flat, anger wants to spring upright, my whole body longs to speak in motion rather than word. So I step away from the structure, not the brotherhood. Coffee with Mark, hikes with José, midnight calls with Caleb keep the connective tissue intact. I leave the frame but carry the men with me.

I loved my men's-group brothers and their support, yet a quiet awareness kept surfacing: the group's warmth never reached the depth I craved. The organization taught us to meet another's pain with composed neutrality—shoulders loose, faces calm, no visible currents. That practiced stillness wrapped my story like gauze: warm, translucent, but never quite touching the raw marrow where childhood feelings still lodged. I'd seen that same calm in Vida once—and felt the same loneliness beneath it. I wondered—if my grief left them unmoved, was the fault in their training or in my feeling?

My family and I keep our distance—occasional calls, polite updates, nothing that reaches the heart. I no longer visit Pakistan; distance keeps the peace. I told them I wasn't gay, that my confusion came from trauma. They were relieved, but their relief landed as rejection—of me, the person.

Body scans melt into impromptu floor work, free-form dance continues. Journals fall mute while paint surges—colors my mind can't name but my muscles remember. Thought abdicates; following the body becomes proof that I am, unmistakably, alive. Bil and Rafi roam the rooms like twin shadows, then bracket me at night with warm, steady breath—their devotion steadying the new rhythm.

I stop outsourcing truth. I keep what resonates and trust the guidance that wells up—raw bodily instinct unshackled from doctrine.

The journey isn't over, but I am home—and that is enough.

The Vortex

2009

Chapter 19

Age 42

I press my palms to sandstone—
cool, veined, sure.
The rock answers first: a chill seeping through skin and fascia, like
light.
It rides my forearms, slips behind my eyes;
skull loosens, thought unlatches.

Head to spine, I pool in the belly.
Swelling, I flow through thighs into calves;
toes splay, listening, soles sip stone, every nerve lit.

I bloom inward and outward at once:
core embered, limbs rousing, fingers quivering, wrists humming.
Four-point crawl—no effort, only current.
Each hold surfaces on arrival, each ledge greets me as kin.

I do not conquer the rock; we converse.
At the crest I shed all, lie naked, arms wide,
the stone's stored sun flooding me—liquid daylight, one unbroken
body;
If this were the last moment, it would be enough.

Such ease visits now—no longer just once a season, no longer gone before I can exhale the cool scent of rain-washed earth. It drops in daily. I loop the neighborhood on my bike for no reason but joy. Sunlight flickers through oaks like gold dust, and the air is sweet with warm pine and the faint vanilla of blooming alyssum. A burst of citrus still tingles on my tongue from the orange slice I bite at the corner—bright, sharp, alive. Bil and Rafi whirl around me like schoolkids at recess, chasing one another through pools of shifting light.

The old questions still lurk at the horizon, yet these ordinary moments ring louder than the past—enough to keep me moving forward.

That evening I pull up to Caleb's bungalow for a reunion of my old men's group turned potluck. The place is already thrumming—stove-steam fogs the windows, plum-dark wine breathes on the long cedar table, candles sway in the stirred air.

I cross the threshold into easy hands on my shoulders, nods that need no words. These are the men I howl beside, weep beside, trust with the rawest marrow; their nearness threads my pulse into something steady.

Halfway through dinner I find myself beside Tara, a friend-of-a-friend visiting from Santa Cruz, both of us balancing plates of roasted squash, steam rising between us. Her laugh rings low and clear; her questions wait for real answers. Conversation slides from joke to genuine curiosity in a heartbeat.

"So—are you with someone?" she asks, head tilted, voice soft. A faint cinch flutters beneath my ribs. "Not at the moment."

She accepts that, then circles back later: "Was your last relationship serious?"

"Yeah," I say. She leans in. "What was she like?"

My mouth dries. The last relationship is with a man, Adrian. There's no slot on the conversational shelf for that truth. I give her something true but thin. A cool pane drops between us, sound-dampening. From the outside I look engaged; inside, my words knock softly against the glass and slide back.

She tells a story about her roommates; I laugh, but the echo finds nowhere to land. By dessert I realize I've spoken for ten minutes without revealing a single inch that matters. Friendly, smiling, untouchable—that shape keeps me both safe and lonely.

The obstacle isn't Tara's warmth or my courage; it's the culture's narrow map—straight, gay, coupled, seeking. A man who has loved both men and women yet still names himself straight drifts off-map from those cartographies. Without a word for it, part of me stays invisible, even in a room full of people I trust to catch me.

Six of us carpool to Castle Rock, the road winding through redwoods, our talk loose. Mid-afternoon I top a sun-warmed boulder and find Lucia beside me—same car, same laugh, suddenly in focus. Light snares her hair; wind lifts the hem of her tee; my compass snaps north.

She smiles, unhurried. "You climb here often?"

"Recently, yes," I say, my chest widening.

"Want to scout a new line sometime? Coffee after work Thursday?" I ask.

Thursday coffee turns into a rhythm—Saturday breakfasts, midweek bouldering, long porch talks while raccoons rattle the recycling. Two weeks in, we start calling it dating and pick our first all-day adventure: a quiet loop through Henry Cowell Redwoods.

A week later our footfalls are already muted by red-brown needles, the air sugared with sap. Several miles in, a moss-soft clearing ringed by cathedral trunks holds us still. Sunlight spears the canopy in broad gold blades, dust motes drifting like fireflies. Silence feels alive, holding its breath for us.

Her eyes meet mine and something unlatches—a clatter of inner locks. I sink through my soles into the damp earth, then rise, an oak thick with living sap, each ring a record of hunger. Heat slides up the columns of my shins, flooding thighs, belly, ribs, throat. My frame thrums as if bells are ringing in every joint. Beside me she unfurls like a wildflower catching first light, and for a beat the whole forest breathes with us.

Blood pumping in my groin. We shrug off packs, peel away damp layers, and lay ourselves on the cool living floor. When our bodies touch, strength draws upward from soil through my pelvis and spine; every thrust a clean piston stroke, guided by gravity and breath. Her breath braids with mine, pulse answering pulse. The small tilts of her hips send clarion notes through my ribs; our rhythms knit into one unbroken current. Desire and motion strike the same bright spark.

She receives me without flinch or shield, her widening trust enlarging the field in which we move. The more she opens, the steadier my power grows. I meet her gaze, offer silent thanks. Her answering kiss seals the moment—a soft stamp: Yes. I feel it too.

We slip into a quiet cadence: six months of sex nearly every day—sometimes twice—never scheduled, only sparked by a glance or the brush of skin.

More than once, tears spill mid-thrust—freedom's overflow, safe enough to be fierce and undefended at once. She holds the rhythm, meeting my power with her steadiness, until the storm settles into breath.

The first time it happens, she asks why the tears.
I tell her I don't know—only that my body is letting go of what words never could.
She pulls me close, and we just breathe for a while.

I have never been fused so seamlessly to my own flesh. My body sings—musk and warmth and sinew. I roam long trails alone to hear that music more clearly, breathing in the scent rising from my body's heat. And it becomes unmistakable: every man I once chased was a hurried patch for the rift Asif tore between me and my body. Now the seam is gone, and I stand entire.

Sadly, beyond the bedroom our rhythms unravel. She chases midnight sparks and last-minute detours; I wake with first light and kneel to routine. Affection lingers, but permanence never takes root. When we part, the goodbye feels muted, inevitable.

After Lucia, sex with women feels instinctive. I drift through brief connections; desire rises on its own, my body answering without pause. The ease startles me.

I tell myself the work is finished—months of embodied sex with women must have broken Asif's curse. Yet my developmental gaps hum in the background—not one with my body, less than whole, less than a man. I assume more embodied sex will wash it out.

Healing is sedimentary: dissolve one layer, and another rises to the surface. Knots lurk not only in muscle, but in coiled intestines where trauma broods; in a liver thawing from its long freeze; and in bean-shaped kidneys where fear murmurs like groundwater, ready for the faintest quake.

Chapter 20

Age 43

The yoga studio stays at eighty degrees—warm enough for muscles to uncurl. Gauzy curtains soften the light; sandalwood threads the air. Mats stretch edge to edge. When another student slips in, we nudge our mats tighter to make space.

Sona comes in—the instructor I've trained with for five years. Conversations stop mid-sentence; phones slide beneath mats. No icon, no Sanskrit on her charcoal tank.

She scans the rows, nods once. "Phones off. Eyes in." her voice is steady but low. One student hesitates, thumb hovering over the screen. Sona points—
"Back wall—five-minute sit."
He moves, and the room settles.

I've seen it before: firm, never unkind.

We flow through long-held poses with barely a cue. Sona moves among us, a steady current. Her adjustments are rare but exact—hands land with a precision my nerves trust. When her palm finds my rib cage in a deep twist, I don't brace; my body exhales, as if it has been waiting for that touch. Unlike other teachers whose zeal leaves me aching for days, her touch never tips into strain, no matter how deep she guides.

Mid-sequence, as we tremble in Warrior II, Sona speaks without raising her voice. "Integrity isn't what you post on your blog," she says, "it's what you'll lose students over." Her eyes sweep the room. "I skip Sanskrit chants. Stolen, colonized, resold—foreign words won't mend it." One woman rolls up her mat and slips out. Sona doesn't flinch, letting the room settle back into breath and silence.

I am still a little afraid—not of her kindness, but of how firmly she stands in herself. The part of me that collapses under Asif's two-year siege still clenches around authority.

Week after week I return—not because the fear fades, but because my body trusts her hands more than it fears her fire.

After class, a few of us often linger. We drink tea in the small kitchen, share simple meals on the studio's back steps. Sona joins us sometimes.

She talks openly about her own past: the chaos of narcissistic parents, the ways their control shaped her body, the years it took for yoga to help her reinhabit it. Hearing her speak that plainly disarms me. It's the first time I've seen a teacher name trauma openly.

Her openness makes me trust her.

———————————

Hours bent over spreadsheets send a flickering ache up my sacrum; heat packs and stretches fail, so I book the first opening with a chiropractor down the block.

Thin sunlight pools across the waiting room; eucalyptus drifts from a diffuser. He arrives—salt-and-pepper hair, kind eyes, broad shoulders beneath a navy polo—and I follow him in, perfectly at ease.

Paper crackles beneath me, breath steady until his palm finds the rim of my pelvis, thumbs tracing the sacroiliac seams—firm, clinical, exact. A micro-quake ripples, blood surging south into an unwanted erection. I shift, trying to hide it, but the motion only heightens it—heart racing, sweat rising.

He notices only the guarding in my muscles and murmurs, "Stay still."

My body empties out—heart afraid—while my groin sparks with its own current. It's the old Asif pattern lighting up, only now my trained awareness is sharp. I feel the shards of childhood lodged in me—hurting, alone. Love rises for my younger self. I vow to gather every fragment of my childhood and let it live again in my body.

That night I do a long, improvised movement practice—feel what's there and let it move. After, the insight lands clean: I'm spent—done asking women to help me land in my body, exhausted from replaying Asif with other men. I want peace, a solid shore to land on. I need to descend, spelunker-style, into the fault line Asif left—lamp swinging against raw stone—until I give choice and power back to those childhood shards.

A week later, I choose to be with a man again—first time in six years—to watch the trauma-shaped patterns rise and see if my new somatic tools can loosen them.

A message lights the screen: "Six-mile sunset loop? —Vince, 38, runner."
We pace the shoreline path, shoes drumming dirt, conversation threading between breaths. His stride is clean—and when dusk cools the sweat, he steers me toward his apartment.

He brushes his thumb along my jaw and pauses; our eyes lock, heat gathering fast—just as it did with Adrian years ago. Clothes slip away. Breath thickens with promise.
Then my palm meets his chest, and the dream glaze shatters.

His skin—his unmistakably male presence—snaps into focus. For years, I sensed men through the fog of developmental mutilation and sexual trauma, mistaking that pull for connection. I perceived them as disowned parts of myself, hoping that sex—the deepest intimacy possible between two people—might make me feel whole.
Now, with new wiring in my nervous system, the illusion dissolves. For the first time, I see a man as separate from me in intimacy.

What stands before me is not my missing half but another human being. The touch that once felt magnetic now reverses polarity—softly repelling, like matching poles.

I lose arousal and Vince's expression clouds with disappointment. I like him—genuinely—but what moves through me now is friendship, not desire.

He steadies his breath, voice low. "I thought we had a moment. Maybe I read it wrong?"

I tell him the truth—I'm working through something complicated, still figuring things out. I hope we can stay connected, maybe go running again sometime.
He nods, eyes sliding away. "Yeah… maybe," he says, already reaching for his shirt.

Wanting to go deeper—I continue dating men.

Each time, the pattern repeats: pleasurable arousal flares, then snaps off the instant skin meets skin. The deeper the emotional connection, the faster desire dissolves—often before we're even naked. The charge softens; what remains feels platonic, brotherly, safe.

But why the initial arousal?
I realize that I need a vessel sturdy enough to hold that same-sex current at full burn—a private crucible where I can taste its hue, feel its crackle without another man's body closing the circuit. I want to hover beside it, not enact it; to trace it through fascia and marrow, chart its contours, and claim it in the tempo of my own heartbeat.

A gay sex club—the safest and smartest place for me to start.

I lock away my clothes, knot a towel at my hips, and follow men into the spacious steam room. I find a quiet corner near the tiled wall, half veiled in vapor, and settle there.

Bodies move through the mist—some draped in towels, others bare, their forms soft in the haze and low light. The air feels primal—a field of male energy that asks only to be felt. A subtle stir blossoms in my groin. I close my eyes and slip inward, feeling arousal in slow motion. A bead of water slides from temple to chest; I follow its bright thread to my pelvis. I have no desire for touch, only to feel the bodies around me.

I draw on the improvised movement practice from my somatic psychology training—every groove I've ever practiced. Slow squats, push-ups, anything to feel my own strength, to keep my energy from leaking toward them.
I still draw from them, but less as siphoning, more as resonance—letting it wake the primal sense of my own body.

I let the arousal spread through my body. Childhood ice melts, sinking back into marrow. I belong solely to myself.

Outside, the night air is cool, but the ember inside holds its glow. The child-me who once borrowed maleness from others now walks quietly beside me, each step knitting us together.

I slide into the driver's seat, but the churn in my belly says *wait*. I recline, letting the car cradle me. My body begins to release the trauma stored in my organs—burps, sighs, farts. Each ripple thaws a childhood shard, stitching it back into place.

I keep drifting back to gay sex clubs—heart pounding, drawn less to contact than to the clean feeling of being in my body. Curiosity nudges me to try a touch, and the instant my fingers meet another man's skin, the spell breaks. I jolt awake—same as with Vince and the others.

In private, the fantasies grow louder, circling like a predator. I am trapped, pacing the same fevered loop.

Saturday. Henry Cowell Redwoods.
I hike until the trail narrows and the noise falls away. Red trunks stand like pillars. Ferns keep the shade. I move deeper until a ring of trees gathers me. Shirt off. Back to earth—duff soft, bark against my shoulder blades. Birdsong stitches the air. Water counts itself over stone.

I listen from the inside out. The diaphragm unspools. Small sounds slip free—sighs, a low hum, the gut remembering its work. I let them pass; I let the next ones come.

Time loosens. Forest in me; me in the forest. Then it arrives—clean, bright, unmistakable. I sit up, soil on my palms, heart steady.

I know what to do next.

In my Castro days I kept seeing flyers for a weekend retreat for gay and bi men—promising deeper work. The memory surfaces now and pulls me forward. I sign up.

A few hours from the city, the retreat sits in a forested valley—wide meadows, scattered cabins, a clear stream threading the grounds. Gravel crunches under tires, cedar on the air. A hand-lettered sign, a folding table, name tags. From the first moment, warmth: men greeting with easy smiles, a light touch to the shoulder. The welcome feels simple and real.

Workshops dot the grounds—breathwork, partner yoga, poetry—some under open tents, others beneath trees. On a grassy slope men play improv; at the fire circle they trade stories. I drift, unsure what I'm seeking but certain I'll know it when it comes.

Down a shaded path beneath redwoods, men kneel on blankets, massaging shoulders and thighs in a slow, shared rhythm. I watch, then join—one can give, receive, or both. When a man offers, I choose to receive.

I lie face-down on the table, eyes shut. The moment his palms sink, pleasure unfurls—liquid fire seeping through every nerve. My awareness drifts at the edge of sleep as he kneads the inner seam of my thighs; a bright pulse ignites in my groin, thick and undeniable. He lingers, deliberate, circling the center of arousal.

I tell him not to touch my genitals. I float on a tide of raw sensation. The current surging through me is the same one abuse once carved—just touch, and charge, the rest of my body gone. But this time it happens in safety, under my own command. My body recreates the old conditions, but now draws a new boundary—no genital touch.

In the weeks that follow, I chase the feeling—signing up for more sessions with the same group in San Francisco. Each one puts my body back in the same state it knew with Asif: focus on the pleasure, check out from the body, endure.

I don't realize I'm caught in the trauma vortex, unable to find my way out. Until now, my healing hasn't touched the core.

I drift from the things that once anchored me. Long rides become chores; the trail no longer calls. Even walks with Bil and Rafi dwindle. When we do go out, it feels like a task, not our old shared joy. I blame simple tiredness, but a deeper fatigue is taking hold.

My body begins to protest—joints stiffen, breath tightens, nights swell with acid and restless heat. I visit the doctor; every test comes back normal. On paper I'm fine, but inside I feel trapped, depleted.

Deep in my chest, a distant war drum pounds with each heartbeat, impossible to ignore. Each breath grows tighter, the walls inching closer. If I don't act soon, something vital might slip out of reach. I'm caught in the loop—addicted. Life keeps slipping through my hands. Sometimes, I think of Sona—how she healed her trauma with yoga.

I take a six-month leave from work and find a small cedar cottage in Aptos, a short walk from the redwood trails of the Forest of Nisene Marks.

First Contact

2011

Chapter 21

Age 44

I decide to see Sona for private yoga sessions.

Her studio sits tucked behind her house. Each time I arrive, Lucy—her poodle—greets me first, racing to the door, tail thumping, body vibrating with joy. She presses her snout into my palm as if we've been apart for years, then rolls onto her back. I kneel, bury my face in her warm chest. When she springs up again, she licks my cheeks clean.

The studio is a playground for the body. Props line one wall: well-worn blocks, bolsters, blankets, and straps. A sling hangs from the ceiling, ready to cradle someone upside down like a bat exhaling into space. Dumbbells rest in rows beside resistance bands. In the corner, a basket spills over with bouncy balls and stuffed animals—oddities anywhere else, yet perfectly at home here.

A floor-to-ceiling glass window turns the studio into a quiet lookout. Redwoods lift beyond the pane while a stream whispers over stones, its bubbling percussion drifting inside. Ferns shimmer in the breeze; light pulses across their fronds. Earth, water, and air aren't backdrop but braid, woven into movement and stillness.

Seeing her here—home, trees, water—my body is welcome. It's a stark contrast to a therapist's office: not sit-and-talk. Here I move. I hang in the sling, crawl, shake, press into blocks. Lucy settles by the mat, tail thumping. The creek keeps a low rhythm. Redwoods hold the edges of my sight. We let the body lead and put words second.

By our fourth session I feel safe with her. I remind her she'd mentioned healing through yoga and ask if I can share my childhood trauma—maybe she can help.

"Of course," she says.

I fold onto the mat. She mirrors me, sitting cross-legged. Her gaze holds mine—soft, unwavering.

I let out a long breath. "A twenty-nine-year-old man sexually abused me for two years when I was thirteen."

She leans back until her shoulders rest against the wall—drawing on the steadiness to keep from pitching forward. The gesture isn't retreat but mooring, setting her keel so she can absorb the freight I unload into the space between us. One slow breath blossoms through her ribs, and in that rise her whole bearing realigns—teacher softening into witness.

Her eyes never leave mine. They shimmer, not with alarm but with unarmored sorrow vast enough to carry the story's weight. A single tear gathers, slips free; she lets it travel. Her jaw quivers, then settles; the muscles of her throat work to stay open. It is the face of a mourner watching a flag fold over a coffin—shock braided with grief and a fierce refusal to look away.

Her body receives the news; the resonance travels through her tone, her breath, her eyes—reaching the frozen places in me, warming what went numb at thirteen.

I feel the first splinters loosen, drift, then slip into the channels I've spent a decade carving with breath, movement, and stubborn will. What has been locked in separate, aching pieces begins to move.

"I'm so sorry," she breathes. "No one should have to live through that."

I didn't know this was the hunger driving me: the clear, unwavering mirror of empathy—ordinary as breath, vital as water, yet in most of life, achingly rare.

My fragmented childhood melts—the floodgates blow open.
Tremors rattle my ribs; sobs hitch in hiccupping bursts as time washes away.
Without turning I feel her warmth settle beside me; inner locks slip free.
She inches closer, her palm resting between my shoulder blades, heat pooling at the back of my heart.
When the torrent eases, she asks—"Who hurt you? Where was your family? How did it begin?"

Her voice stays level. The questions matter to her as much as to me.

This isn't therapy as I know it—it's simple human contact, the kind that rewires. One body staying open while another trembles—that's how healing begins.

That night, I sleep twelve hours straight, my body wrung out from the inside. My intestines churn, organs throb. I cry often; each tear releases another measure of peace—soft, unforced.

Next session.
We sit cross-legged on our mats. I open my mouth to name what Asif has done—skin goes numb, thoughts scatter.

"Slow down," Sona says, her voice a hand on my spine. "Stay with what you feel."

I breathe, and wait for my body to guide me. How do I share without dissociating? My body goes to plank pose to feel its own strength, to hold the young and afraid parts. This is somatic integration.

From deep in my gut, a word ignites—*Fuck no.* Ten push-ups drive it through my muscles, each rep a refusal, a return of strength once taken.

"I will not live in your prison, you bastard!" The sentence rings through bone like a bell, a *no* I did not feel at thirteen.

Sona nods. "Keep the anger moving—feel it."

I do squats, kicks, resistance bands—rage excavating every corner. Asif's prison cell collapses; movement floods the ground.

Sona is not a therapist. What she does comes from her own understanding of somatic psychology and yoga, not from formal clinical training. Still, what happens between us feels more healing than anything I experience in therapy.

I had worked with therapists who described themselves as somatic, but none had offices like hers—spaces where I could move, cry, shake. The moment I stepped into a therapist's office, a hierarchy took shape: therapist and client. Those roles, even when well-intentioned, created a distance that blocked the natural connection between two people.

With Sona, that hierarchy doesn't exist. We meet as equals—human to human—and something in that openness allows real healing to happen. Sona tells me she has never done anything like this with another client, and that, in witnessing me process trauma, she learns more about how to work with it. I find creative ways to move through it, and she supports and witnesses.

It is somatic healing at its best—spontaneous, improvised, alive.

Over the next months, our sessions sound like a gym spliced with a den of animals. We begin on the floor—knees scraping, palms thumping—gravity making us equals. A guttural "huh" leaves my chest each time I drive a lunge into the floor. When rage peaks, I let it out in sharp growls, fists slapping against a bolster.

I'm finally finding the anger I couldn't feel as a child—the anger toward those who hurt me. It's settling into my cells and tissues, giving me strength and confidence to live the way I want, instead of pulling me back into trauma-shaped patterns.

I didn't lack skill with Sona. Years of Vipassana and somatic practice had trained me to access that depth. But the catalyst was empathy. Even with all the training, I needed another human's heart to meet what I couldn't feel alone—to recognize it, validate it, and let it thaw and release.

At first light I lace my shoes and slip into the red-bark gorge of The Forest of Nisene Marks. Every stride slaps the earth like a paddle, calves frothing with heat. Breath runs glass-clear, heart laughing, as though each footfall sinks a root deeper. Ten miles on, at Santa Rosalia Overlook two thousand feet above tidewater, I feel like the Indus—steady in flow, immense in strength.

Chapter 22

The six months in Aptos unfurl like one long inhalation beneath the canopy of the Nisene redwoods. At dawn, I run the fern-slick trails with Rafi and Bil; at dusk, I hike until the light turns copper and the forest exhales its cool resin. Every week—sometimes twice—I sit with Sona, peeling back each calcified layer of memory until raw veins of truth pulse in the space between us. Day after day, the solitude pours clean weight into my limbs: lungs widen, stride lengthens, sinew knits itself stronger. Confidence glows in my body like sap rising after fire.

I return to Pakistan to see Father and Ashi. Eight years have passed since Mother's death. Father has retired. He'd never kept friends, and the long quiet has done its sanding—loneliness rounding the hard edges that once defined him.

Days pass in small reunions and formal meals, everything polite, held together. Then one night, the house sleeps. I slip the latch at two in the morning after meeting old friends. Hinges whine; lights stay dark.

Footsteps. My father charges down the hall, barking like I'm still a teenager under his roof. "It's two in the morning! Why

so late?"
Nothing in me stirs. I'm surprised by my own calm.

I don't see him as I did when I was young. Now I see a
frightened man. His tirade runs a few minutes; I let it pass.

"Dad," I say when the room goes quiet, "I didn't come here to
fight with you."

He blinks, lost; the anger has nowhere to land. His face folds.
He cries. He steps in and holds me. I hold him back. My chest
shakes; the years loosen.

After that night, he begins to call. For seven more years—until
he died—he calls to tell me he loves me. I let it in, visit him
most years. I don't step on the tripwires—Samira, Asif, anything
about my sexuality. I just let the goodness flow.

Over time, Ashi softens. Nimra too.

With Huma, the wall holds. Her husband won't speak about his
brother; to keep the peace, she stays quiet. They want silence
from me too. I step back. Keeping a relationship on those terms
hurts more than letting it go.

One afternoon, I call Asif. My body shakes; feet planted. The
words come hot and clear—I spare no profanities. I ask how
many others. I ask if he's gotten help, what he will do to take
responsibility. He keeps saying, "I'm sorry," until the words
turn hollow. No answers.

I end the call.

I return to work in Mountain View and let the rhythm of office elevators and humming servers fold around me again.

That's when he shows up—Zak, the new guy on our team: sharp-minded, athletic—and, yes, handsome. The kind of man who, not long ago, would make me vanish. Someone I'd study too closely, siphoning from his presence.

As I close my laptop, he leans over the cubicle wall—voice easy, eyes holding mine a second longer than needed.

"I'm grabbing lunch at a little Mediterranean spot a block away. Join me?"

"Sure."

We walk the first few minutes in easy silence, sun warming our backs, traffic humming. At the café he opens the door and steps aside, something unreadable flashing across his face—half invitation, half habit.

Inside smells of grilled meat and lemon. We order and take the window table. We talk—where we grew up, what brought us here. His gaze lingers, then slips away.

I keep my answers light, voice even, hands folded. Under the table, a low current runs through me. I notice how he listens, how he looks down right when I look up, as if avoiding being caught. When I ask about him, he stays general—weekend runs, a housemate, friends in the neighborhood. No names. No pronouns to trip over.

The food arrives and the talk thins, not awkward—just charged. He wipes his mouth, smiles, eyes softer now.

"Next time," he says, "I'll pick somewhere with better seating."

Something in his tone carries more than lunch—enough warmth to register, not enough to confirm. I nod, studying the check.

On the walk back he matches my pace. At the crosswalk our sleeves brush; he laughs at something small and too quickly. Near the lobby he holds the door and says, "Good to have you on the team." The words are ordinary. The look isn't.

As before, my feet begin to go numb—energy draining toward him, my center of gravity sliding outside my skin. On our walk back to the office, I focus within my body, make sure that my attention does not bleed toward Zak.

I breathe.

The anger I've braided into my cells and tissues fires. A living armor forms—cellular, primal, organic—something that should have grown in early childhood, declaring that my life belongs to me, not to my parents. An energetic immune system clicks in—my body saying, *not this time.*

Strength rises through my soles, threading upward, weaving my body back together. A hint of swagger follows—subtle arm swing, quiet bicep curl.

We break apart toward our desks.

My relationship with Zak stays professional. For a while, he continues his stealthy interest, and I use it as an opportunity to pull the current that reaches out to him back into my body—another thread of childhood finding its way home. In time, Zak's interest settles into simple collegial ease.

Months pass, teaching me how my body can answer differently. Around men, attraction slow-burns to life in my body. Around women, I radiate a coltish ease, a boyish blush I no longer hide. Same-sex fantasies evaporate. On weekends I torch personal records up the Bay Area's most challenging climbs—Mount Umunhum, Mount Hamilton—any road pointing skyward. Confidence at work soars—my voice carries, posture unshaken. And, most important, fear no longer lodges beneath my ribs.

I invite my men's group buddies—Caleb, José, and Mark—for dinner. We haven't gathered since my Aptos exodus. Dusk pools at the windows as we drift inside, savoring desserts. I tell them: the redwoods, sessions with Sona, the moment with Zak when I don't collapse. Mark gives a low whistle, Caleb nods. We melt into the couches.

José leans forward, elbows on his knees. "You've been through a lot—some beautiful, some rough. Say more."

"At its core, my healing wasn't about sex at all. It was about meeting the boy I once was—reaching back to those first fifteen years with empathy: holding him, letting him try what he'd longed to do, now with an adult's safety. Letting him have his yeses and his nos. Reminding him that none of it was ever his fault.

It meant integrating the capable adult I had built with that younger self. With support, I gently and consciously re-entered my muted childhood so my body could finally move through what it couldn't then.

My body split maleness from sexuality to survive. I felt sexual pleasure during the years when sexuality should have been weaving itself into my muscles and tissues. The split ran deep. As an adult, it felt as though embracing my maleness fully would mean losing the ability to have sex."

The quiet holds us. I steady my breath and continue.

"I often wonder what it would be like to feel natural attraction during my teenage years. To be curious with confidence. To explore my manhood in a way that belongs to me. I'll never know. That's the isolating, lifelong loss many of us who grow up like this carry. And sometimes I wonder—can anyone who grew up safe ever truly understand the depth of that loss?"

José's eyes are moist. He nods slowly, then leans forward and wraps his arms around me. His chest is warm—no words, just pressure and breath.

Mark follows, then Caleb. One by one they fold in; no one rushes to fix or name what's just been shared. Someone's wet cheek brushes mine—and I realize mine is wet, too.

I feel them holding not just me, but the boy who never gets to cry in someone's arms.
This time, I don't disappear; I stay.

Chapter 23

Silence settles like dusk among cedars—no melody but the calm of dogs at rest and the last exhale of light across the floorboards. Bare soles kiss the cool grain; one palm rests over my sternum, the other floats loose as a frond. Nothing elaborate—simply standing, letting life ripple outward like circles on a lake.

For years, the left side of my body carried more charge—not stronger, just overworked. The right side lagged, half absent. Two knots held the split: one buried in the pelvis, the other lodged where skull meets spine.

But this evening, something shifts.
Weight distributes evenly into both feet. The right side no longer lags; the left releases its constant guard. The base of my skull softens; the bowl of my pelvis unclenches. The knots loosen into warmth, and energy moves freely up my spine.

This was the want beneath all wants—to rest in my body. Not sex, not a banner of orientation.
Enough.
Satisfied.
Whole.
Complete.

From this hush, coupling with anyone—any body, any gender—feels like stepping out of the room of my ribs—I'd rather stay, to meet others from here—no grasping, only company—while I keep my shape.

Even after the breakthrough, my body still replays its old pattern—a tremor at the ribs, breath catching short, the pelvic floor snapping shut. Desire flares to fuse with a man, but awareness interrupts before habit can pull me back into reflex.

Integration requires a gut-deep renovation. I keep companions who respect boundaries and step back from those who don't. New relationships form slowly, at a pace my body can trust.

Movement adjusts with need—yoga when joints ask for space, biking when lungs want air, stillness when only breath will do. Even food changes: eating becomes listening. Each meal either settles or unsettles me, and I pay attention to every signal.

Sometimes during improvised practice, the movements are tiny, invisible from the outside—feeling for where childhood fear has set like cement. I stay with the sensation. Soon enough, a new **body → feeling → story** path begins to form; the fear loosens and flows through the new channel.

Nearing forty-five, I keep asking why healing took so long. At thirty, I enter therapy and return weekly, naming every shard I can reach.

Spring 2013. Hours after the Boston Marathon finish line comes apart, I walk into a neighborhood café. The flatscreens don't blink. They loop the blast—shockwave, a runner folding, a sneaker pinwheeling through smoke. Beneath it, a silent crawl counts the dead from a Damascus market bombing. The barista mutes the feed so soft indie heartbreak can keep crooning over the hiss of milk. No one objects. We protect the vibe.

I feel the grief rise—small, private. Eyes wet. No one meets them. A manager calls "next," and the line snaps forward.

Outside, a man sets up—a crate, a paper cup, a sign. Music from the café leaks onto the street. People give him coins without giving him eyes.

It isn't just today. We've trained ourselves to mute what hurts if it doesn't hurt us.

I walk toward home, each step translating recent headlines into bone: drone strike, austerity cut, marathon blast, foreclosure, rape case dismissed.
A nation can tune out burning cities—why would it pause for an invisible bruise on a boy?

We built a culture for survival, polish, and possession—not for human need or well-being. We serve a system that rewards productivity over aliveness. It trains us to sand down our needs, to trade empathy for efficiency—hearts on mute until the quotas clear. The same machine that breeds trauma sells the anesthetic and calls it wellness.

Hours later, back in bed, the slogans rise uninvited—snippets from books, podcasts, weekend retreats: *Identify with pain and you can't be free of it. Anger, resentment, irritation—your ego in disguise. Your ego survives by comparing itself to others.*
Line after line insists the flaw lives inside me, never in the

world that breeds fracture and then sells the salve. Almost every therapist, teacher, or influencer delivered the same verdict, sometimes blunt, sometimes velvet-wrapped: *You are the problem. Fix yourself so you can slide back into the machine.* That framing blames the individual while erasing the context that harms us. It overlooks the factories of ego, trauma, and control built into our streets, classrooms, and pay stubs.

I open the notebook where I've recently jotted a private definition, meant only for me: *I experience wholeness when my body can feel and speak without being edited for social compliance.*

I feel the mask I once bartered for belonging press back—its edges bruising the very skin it was meant to protect. The ache exposes the bargain: comfort over truth. Breathing into that sting, I loosen the seams and step, however unsure, toward daylight that promises to meet me unguarded.

The next morning, sunlight pools across the stone floors of the Santa Clara County Hall of Justice. I take my numbered badge—Juror #53—and follow the usher into Department 24. Seventy of us fan out across rigid pews that still smell of lemon polish.

The case, the judge explains, involves allegations of child sexual abuse. A hum passes through the room: papers shuffle, throats clear. My pulse ticks once at each wrist—left, then right—but stays steady.

Voir dire begins. One by one, prospective jurors stand, recite name, neighborhood, occupation. Then comes the prosecutor's question: "Have you—or anyone close to you—experienced sexual abuse?" Several heads shake. When my turn arrives, I rise, palms moist against my slacks.

"Juror fifty-three," the clerk prompts.
"Yes," I hear myself say, voice carrying farther than expected. "I was sexually abused as a child."
No tremor, no heat rising up my neck. Just a statement of fact, round and solid.

The prosecutor nods. "Could you remain impartial in this case?"
"No, sir. I cannot."

The judge thanks me for my honesty and excuses me. Footsteps drum on polished wood, a door eases shut behind me. The whole exit takes maybe ten seconds, but it feels like a mile of open air.

In the hallway, a young man—juror badge still clipped to his jacket—jogs up, breath hitching. "Hey—thank you for saying that," he whispers.

I nod, throat thick. "You're welcome" slips out.

He returns to the courtroom; I walk toward the escalators, knees suddenly light. Outside, street traffic roars its usual indifference, but something inside shifts—quiet, definite—as if a sealed room finally breathes.

A month later, just a few hours before the birthday gathering I'm hosting, I get up and pad to the bathroom. I've invited people I feel grateful to—those who have supported me at different turns—along with anyone they wish to bring. On the counter lies the shirt I've bought for the occasion: soft and breathable. Before dressing, I pause, naked, in front of the mirror.

The man in the mirror carries the outline I once hunted in others—lean torso narrowing clean to the waist, legs thick from miles of climb, glutes rounding with the quiet force of river-hewn boulders.

Chapter 24

Lanterns loop the backyard like a low constellation—bee-gold bulbs hang from camellia to railing, light pooling on faces I have gathered with equal parts gratitude and daring. Caleb steers the portable speaker by the grill, shifting from indie folk guitars to midnight blue R&B, while Mark has already set a tier of cupcakes on the patio table. Sohail laughs about yoga with Sona; José nurses a mason jar of lemonade beside the herb planters.

As dusk thickens, warmth gathers low in my belly and rises through my spine. My legs feel steady under me, weight spreading evenly through the soles of my feet. Breath deepens; ribs expand. A quiet current moves through the body, calm and alive at once. I drift from cluster to cluster, each unhurried hug landing heart to heart. By the time I reach the patio table, I am both anchored and open—balanced from feet to crown, every cell saying yes.

Forty-five.

A coworker presses a mug of stout into my hand.

"Happy birthday," she says, eyes bright. "You invited half the building."

I smile. "The ones I love working with."

A breeze teases the lantern cords, and Caleb lowers the music. Mark lights a circle of candles on the cupcake tier; each wick catches a golden bloom. Conversations thin to a hush as he carries the tray toward me, flames pirouetting above vanilla frosting.

"Time for a wish," he says. Someone dims the string lights, and the candles bloom into the only stars.

Friends and coworkers form a loose horseshoe. My chest unfurls on its own.

"My wish," I say, "is simple: that we all tell the truest story we know and still belong."

I draw one steady breath and say:

"I was sexually abused for years, starting at thirteen. That wound confused everything, especially desire. I kept turning to men, looking for clarity, until my body finally told the truth: I'm whole when my desire turns to women."

Silence, then a collective exhale.

"Thank you," I add, meeting every gaze. "You helped me get here."

José raises his lemonade, Sona presses a hand to her heart. I bend, blow out the candles in one unbroken stream, and the dark fills with applause gentle enough not to break anything—only to seal what has just begun.

Survivor Resources

A small constellation of resources lies ahead, ready to light your way.

For Male Sexual Violence
1in6 https://1in6.org
Men Healing https://www.menhealing.org
Male Survivor https://malesurvivor.org

Somatic Psychology
NARM https://narmtraining.com
Somatic Experiencing https://traumahealing.org